Religion and Generation Z

Why seventy per cent of young people say they have no religion

A collection of essays by students

Religion and Generation Z

Why seventy per cent of young people
say they have no religion

A collection of essays by students

Edited by Brian Mountford

CHRISTIAN ALTERNATIVE
BOOKS

Winchester, UK
Washington, USA

JOHN HUNT PUBLISHING

First published by Christian Alternative Books, 2022
Christian Alternative Books is an imprint of John Hunt Publishing Ltd.,
No. 3 East St., Alresford, Hampshire SO24 9EE, UK
office@jhpbooks.com
www.johnhuntpublishing.com
www.christian-alternative.com

For distributor details and how to order please visit the 'Ordering' section on our website.

Text copyright: Brian Mountford 2021

ISBN: 978 1 78904 931 2
978 1 78904 932 9 (ebook)
Library of Congress Control Number: 2021936363

A CIP catalogue record for this book is available from the British Library.

Design: Stuart Davies

UK: Printed and bound by CPI Group (UK) Ltd, Croydon, CR0 4YY
Printed in North America by CPI GPS partners

We operate a distinctive and ethical publishing philosophy in all areas of our business, from our global network of authors to production and worldwide distribution.

Contents

The biggest junk yard in history is the one marked *Abandoned Religions*, abandoned because they are incapable of adapting to the flowing currents of human history... That resistance to change is one reason for their decline amongst many young people today. The so-called millennial generation, both in the UK and in the USA, is the least religiously committed cohort of the population there has been in the last sixty years... There is still a spiritual hunger and interest among the young, but they show a marked contempt for institutions which claim that they alone can perfectly satisfy it.

Richard Holloway, *Waiting for the Last Bus*, Canongate Books, 2018

To be rationally sustainable, religions must ally with the best modern science and with textual criticism; they must accept that ancient moral rules must often be adapted to new circumstances and that they should be conducive to universal human flourishing; they must attempt to find some plausible general world-view within which religions can find a place; they must adopt an informed global and historically conscious outlook; and they should accept that conceptual descriptions of ultimate reality are not free of local and changing linguistic and cultural influences.

Keith Ward, *Religion in the Modern World*, CUP, 2019

List of Contributors

Brian Mountford

Brian has been a priest for fifty years, most of which has been spent working in Oxford, where he was Vicar of the University Church and Chaplain of St Hilda's College, and Cambridge, where he was Fellow and Chaplain of Sidney Sussex College. The point of this collection of essays is to hear young people in the 18–24-year-old age group say in their own words why seventy per cent of them have 'no religion'. He has edited the volume and topped and tailed it with essays of his own which try to place the contributions in a broader context.

Tara Lee

Brought up in the complex mixture of cultures and belief-systems of Hong Kong, Tara Lee was a cradle Catholic for whom God became a hollow word. She toyed with the ecumenical idea that we all believe in the same God but found this too bland. Falling in love caused her to re-visit her religious roots where she found momentary consolation. As a talented student of literature, she finds hints of transcendence in aesthetic experience but is content that it is part of what we are, rather than evidence of the divine other.

In this brief but brilliant essay she provides a broad ranging intellectual critique of Christianity and religions which explains much of why her generation identifies as having 'no-religion', even though most of them would not be able to express it.

Christopher T. Bennett

Christopher read theology at Cambridge and is culturally Christian but has no religious commitment. He appreciates that this puts him in a very weird position, as someone who is sympathetic to religion without really being part of one. He laments the fact his contemporaries don't seem to understand and think of theology more as a set of exhausted metaphysical ideas. His background means that his unique selling point is that he can be a 'secular defender of the faith', sometimes trying to convince others of the virtues in religion, while aiming to understand why it is that modern British society has seemingly lost all religion. He notes the cultural shift in Britain over the past century, from a point where the Christian religion was normative to the present in which 'no-religion' has become the default position. He attributes the widespread apathy towards religion in modern Britain among the 18–25-year-old age group to this altered default position, with the consequences that religion has not been actively rejected, but also that there is no clear way for it to re-assert itself due to its reduced stature in cultural consciousness.

Matthew Murphy

Raised a Catholic in Enniskillen, County Fermanagh, Matthew Murphy discovered a new breadth of religious freedom through the musical life of his Oxford college chapel and was surprised to find how many of his contemporaries, while not traditionally religious, were attracted to a spirituality via formal liturgy and aesthetically satisfying music.

His essay explores this and looks further into what he calls a theology of the arts. Now he is working in Coventry Cathedral, where in the 1960s, a thoroughly modern cathedral was built beside the medieval one destroyed by German bombs in World War II. The experience gives him hope for the future of Christianity.

Rumana Ali

Rumana describes growing up as a Muslim in the socially deprived East London Borough of Newham and the cultural religious assumptions this engendered. When at 18 she became an undergraduate at St Hilda's College, Oxford, most of these assumptions were challenged by contemporaries from secular atheist backgrounds. The experience was both alienating and isolating and a powerful illustration of what it means to be religious in the 'no-religion' generation.

Kizzy Jugon

Kizzy's university story is dominated by a sort of ambivalent love hate relationship with Christianity, exacerbated by her sense of its innate hostility towards women. As a feminist she is outraged by this injustice and an experience of sexual assault by a member of the church brings a crisis to her life.

In this feisty piece, she dramatically illustrates one of the principal reasons women in her age group (and in other age groups too, of course) take up the no-religion banner, namely the prejudice against women in the Bible that they are second class. This has surely underpinned the attitude to women in the societies of the Western World.

Despite a breakdown which caused her to drop out of her medical course for three years, Kizzy didn't give up her religion. She discovered there were many examples of liberated women in the Bible, from Ruth to Mary the mother of Jesus, and the new confidence this discovery brought enabled her to live as a Christian.

Nora Baker

The cross-cultural effect of globalisation changes religious attitudes. We see an example of this between Eire (the Republic of Ireland), a Catholic country amidst the Protestant countries of England, Northern Ireland, Scotland and Wales. Nora Baker's take on religion is rooted in the experience of two cultures, which she explores in this essay. In a completely different way from his, her argument supports Christopher Bennett's theory that a major factor in the emergence of the no-religion generation is the cultural marginalisation of religion in secular Britain.

Nora is a DPhil candidate in Oxford's Faculty of Medieval and Modern Languages.

Ben Winchester

Ben is a physicist and he tackles the question of science and religion. He recognises that many of his contemporaries reject religion because they see it as intellectually challenged by science. This is partly because conservative religion, in seeking to defend itself against such a challenge, has tended to present its doctrines as empirical facts and its history, and that of the New Testament, as an account of what actually happened, without the nuance of interpretation, poetry and symbolism. Ben considers doubt and questioning to be a foundational part of science and religion too. Thus, the two disciplines are complementary and mutually helpful.

Hannah Taylor

Hannah has called her piece 'Faith vs Organised Religion' and emphasised therefore that key difference between personal spirituality and the much more prescriptive nature of organised religion. Organised religion has let her down and she is left grappling with how to deal with a persistent personal religiosity that refuses to go away.

Hannah read Chemistry at Oxford and now teaches in a secondary school.

Connie Tongue

Connie Tongue writes a passionate and polemical piece about the Church's failure, as she sees it, to be prophetic on the matter of fossil fuels and climate change. In order to keep their adherents happy, and with the notable exception of Pope Francis, she thinks the churches take an ambivalent and compromising view of the greatest crisis of our day, allowing people to take either side of the argument. She claims her generation is disaffected with the Church's hypocrisy and moral ambivalence and that this gives a reason to ignore the claims of religion.

Keynote Essay

By Brian Mountford

No view of religion in contemporary Britain can ignore the latest data (2017) on religious affiliation, from NatCen's British Social Attitudes survey, that 53%[1] of the people in Britain say they have 'no religion' and that of those, 70%[2] of the 18–25 age-group claim to have no religion. I can amplify this stark statistic anecdotally. In October 2018, I was Acting Chaplain of Corpus Christi College, Oxford, and my first encounter with the new intake of students was at the introductory 'Welfare' meeting, where I faced an auditorium full of eighteen-year-olds looking at me challengingly from seats tiered as steeply as the Colosseum. When I stood up to speak, I sensed intuitively that I must begin by acknowledging we live in a multifaith society, an international society, a post-religious society, where 70% of their age group in the UK claim to have no religion. The sight of nodding heads made me more relaxed. Thus, I acknowledged the unwritten terms and conditions on which I was to act as Chaplain.

In St Hilda's College, where for a long time I was part-time Chaplain, the room designated as the chapel has been demolished as part of a major re-development programme and replaced with a multifaith space. Why should Christianity, and Anglicanism in particular, be privileged in contemporary, secular society? Today, if you were building a college from scratch, would you include a chapel at all? Many of the objectors of course never ever attended a chapel event and some blandly assumed, in a Dawkins-like way, that what goes on there is a sinister attempt at brainwashing, the promotion of irrational belief in impossible things. Had there been a historic chapel building and world class choir the argument wouldn't so easily have progressed and, maybe, the aesthetic virtues of uplifting

1

music would have been seen as self-authenticating and as transcending the perceived small-mindedness of theology. It is clear Christianity as a default, as a norm, is gone, even in Oxford University where, until the mid-nineteenth century, you had to be a member of the Church of England in order either to teach or study there.

No Religion

This collection of essays attempts to shed some light on why so many young people say they have 'no religion'. It does not pretend to be a systematic study, more a series of snapshots that arose from discussions I had with students while I was Acting Chaplain at Corpus Christi College. This is not as parochial as it might sound. Students come to Oxford from all over the world – it is a very international place – and therefore the content helps to understand how young people respond to religion on a much wider base than one city or one country.

On the one hand, my experience with the new students suggests they embrace the term as a reasonable description of their generation; on the other, no-religion can be a misleading term invented for the sociologist of religion's questionnaire, a catch-all category at the end of a multiple-choice question on religious allegiance. No religion does not therefore indicate an active position but a passive one; this is a category I end up in when other options fail. It is more a position of neutrality than an anti-religion statement.

It indicates that a high percentage of 18–25s are indifferent to religion and probably have scarcely brushed against it, particularly in Britain and much of Europe where religion is culturally marginalised. Yet there is much more religion in society than accounted for in sociological surveys, from the footballer who crosses himself when he comes onto the field of play to the motivating power of religion in, for example, American elections and certain national identities, like Israel or Iran. Rumana Ali's essay, however, highlights the difference between different religious cultural backgrounds. In Britain, it is the Christian heritage that has been secularised and marginalised, while the religions of ethnic immigrant communities such as Islam and Hinduism flourish and are passed down between generations.

Beyond that is another subtlety which makes it difficult to argue religion has been eradicated from sections of society – the intuitive sense of there being something metaphysical which lies behind so much of what is loosely referred to as spiritual. Martin Rees, the Astronomer Royal, talking of our cosmic habitat says that 'the pre-eminent mystery is why anything exists at all'. It is such a fundamental question that just trying to imagine nothing at all stretches the mind beyond its limits, because you can only think of nothing in relation to your experience of something. Nothing means no time, no space, no meaning, ever. There is no point of reference for nothing. This is one of the questions that provides raw material for theology. The philosopher John Gray is on to something similar when he says that, while he is both non-religious and anti-atheist, he wants to argue that our innate need to explain mortality and suffering with imagination and myth is far too fundamental to ignore religion. 'I don't have an idea of God or anything but I find the idea that you could wipe the slate clean of that impulse to be ridiculous... Myth-making has been a part of every single human culture in history, why would we imagine that it is disappearing from our own?' (*Observer*, 25 October 2020). It is a view supported by the Israeli historian Yuval Noah Harari who says 'most people think in stories... we live inside the dreams of dead people; all the religions and ideologies and nations and economic theories came out of dreams of people who lived thousands of years ago' (Today Programme, BBC, 12 November 2020). This is not a negative judgement, but a description of how things are. We must live in dialogue with our history. We can do no other. The danger for religious institutionalism is that it is tempted not to allow dialogue but wants to freeze its doctrinal position at some random point of religious evolution.

Those interested in theology will recognise that this kind of argument is not new but was promoted at the beginning of the nineteenth century, during the Enlightenment, by the German protestant theologian Friedrich Schleiermacher. Professor Keith Ward neatly sums up Schleiermacher's position: 'Instead of being founded on a past revelation of inerrant doctrines, he proposed that authentic religious belief begins with a distinctive sort of "intuition" and "feeling". This is an experience of "the infinite" in and through finite things and events' (*Religion in the Modern World*, CUP, 2019).

The essays that follow are by well-educated people who have encountered religion in their upbringing and have variously rejected it, grappled with it, or embraced it. The task I set them, which is by no means the adopted structure for each, was to describe their experience of religion, their view of what their contemporaries think about it, and finally to have a shot at evaluating the future of religion. I found it difficult, however, to get anyone to write from what I called the 'couldn't-care-less' point of view; which wasn't altogether surprising since no one cared enough to be bothered to write it. Yet, it seems likely this stance represents a high proportion of the 70%, not because of animosity towards religion, but through extreme unfamiliarity with it. If your parents don't practise religion, your school doesn't teach it, social media ignores it, the church in the high street looks down at heel, there is no peer group pressure to belong to a religion, then why would you get involved? It is not so different from someone raised in Communist China who has no belief in God because the education system and culture make being an atheist normative.

Eighteen years is a short time to form a person, however long it seems to the growing child. Having experienced the complex drama of becoming yourself, at eighteen you feel you have been through a lot and are ready for the world. If that formative period has been untouched by any kind of religious nurture you will very likely be indifferent if you come across it. This generation has grown up since the Millennium, 9/11, advanced globalisation and the climate crisis. Until the restrictions of the COVID-19 pandemic brought things to a temporary halt, it has been a time of such internationalism and inter-cultural mingling that when people have considered religions, they have seen them as multi-faith options, culturally relative and less definitive than hitherto. Thus, I conclude the primary characteristic of 'no religion' is *unfamiliarity*.

Its second characteristic, I think, is *rationalism*, centred on the empirical scientific argument that the existence of God cannot be proved. For Judaism, Christianity, and Islam this is deeply problematic because their monotheistic belief in the God of Abraham is a defining creedal position and for Christianity, at least, the emphasis on creeds tends to lead to a philosophical and definitional approach to religion.

Whereas in the East, Buddhism, Confucianism, and Taoism are non-theistic, and Hinduism is henotheistic, meaning that while they worship Brahma as principal god, other gods and goddesses have high importance. In the Taoist paradigm of the world, the life force is named chi. Chi is the spiritual essence and force, which flows within and throughout all of existence. Humans have chi, plants and animals have chi, the Earth as a whole has chi as does the greater universe. I think one of the fundamental religious experiences is to have an intuitive sense of an energising life force or spirit and it is part of the raw material contributing to the idea of god.

Eastern religions seem more comfortable with being ragged round the edges, particularly where various local and imported religions, introduced through migration and colonialism, have been syncretised. Vietnam is a classic example, where local ancestor worship is shaped and broadened by Buddhism and

Hinduism from the West, Confucianism from the East, and Catholicism from French colonial rule in the nineteenth century. Also, Eastern religion is more communitarian and focused on the family and wider social groups working for the common good, rather than individual salvation. Interestingly, the Oxford English Dictionary takes a Western view in defining religion as 'the belief in and worship of a superhuman controlling power, especially a personal God or gods', whereas in 1915 the eminent social scientist Émile Durkheim gave a much broader description of religion as 'a unified system of beliefs and practices relative to sacred things'.

But for our purposes in these essays the non-existence of God argument is a gamechanger. Its prevalence in Britain, in my view, is closely related to the tendency amongst conservative Christians and Muslims to insist their metaphysical creedal claims and their more supernatural foundational stories be taken literally rather than as works of poetic truth telling.

When it comes to atheism, I make a distinction between the 'hard' and 'soft' view. Hard atheism is campaigning and doctrinaire, intent on eliminating God and religion, exemplified by Richard Dawkins' *The God Delusion* in which, as it happens, he denigrated many of the things most religious people would also want to denigrate: unthinking fundamentalism, the sins of religions in war and sexual abuse, the loony fringes such as snake handlers and so forth. Soft atheism is a more tolerant view involving an intellectual rejection of the idea of God while respecting the faith of those who nevertheless hold to it. One or two of the essayists in this volume fall into the soft atheist category, most obviously theologian Christopher Bennett, but I couldn't find anyone to write an out-and-out atheist essay from a philosophically neutral viewpoint, possibly because those who are not engaged with thinking specifically about religion see little point in entering the discussion.

It would, of course, be misleading to imply that 18–25s

on the streets of Britain are busily discussing the philosophy of religion but they have inevitably, and often unknowingly, absorbed the secular rationalist framework of the twenty-first-century West, which includes a blend of scientific reductionism, individualism, and, when it comes to religion, the influence of Feuerbach, Marx, Freud, and Nietzsche.

While questioning the existence of God is the main intellectual objection to religion amongst this group, one should not overlook the so-called *Problem of Evil*. When I worked briefly at Wellington College in 2020, a school where chapel attendance is required and not altogether objected to, the sixth form was invited to challenge me on religious assumptions and 75% of their questions were variants on why an all-loving and all-powerful God would allow suffering in the world. The other 25% of questions concerned the Church's stance of sexual ethics. The 18–25s take for granted a liberal and inclusive approach to the LGBT+ culture, same sex marriage, gender fluidity, and sex before marriage, seeing these things as a natural expression of what it is to be human, whereas the Church tends to be conservative and panicky about departing from what it regards as the received teachings of Scripture and Tradition. Not only can these teachings appear unreconstructed, belonging to another age, but even more tellingly, frequently unobserved in the lives of many clergy.

Several of the essays draw attention to this and include accounts of distressing personal experience. The disdain for religion in this age group is significantly a result of the fear of moral censure for behaviour they believe to be both normal and right. Traditionally, religious chaplains have been involved with welfare work amongst students, but in recent years I have encountered several situations in Oxford college life where students have protested that welfare ought to be conducted exclusively by professionally trained counsellors and not by religious professionals. The principal objection is fear of moral censure. How can a counsellor be helpful if they are judging you? I entirely see the force of the student argument, although in practice I see many clergy fulfilling this role with neutrality, great empathy, popularity, and compassionate success.

When I discussed this essay with screenwriter Zoe Green, who is a generation older, she pointed out another factor unsurprisingly not identified by the 18–25s: that immaturity and lack of experience might partly explain the higher percentage of young no-religionists. She said that, if you disregard the 'Romeo and Juliet type exceptions', in most cases 18–25s hadn't experienced the mystery of loving a partner or child. But for very many people marriage and early parenthood are times when they take stock of their responsibilities and ask themselves serious questions about life and love, of the kind often dealt with better by literature, art, and religion, than by scientific formulae. At eighteen, without the depth of nuanced experience on which to base your convictions, you tend to be absolutist and instinctive. You see yourself as free and open to anything, but at the same time can be stubbornly defensive about the relativism and fluidity of thought and social attitude which you see as giving you that freedom. This is ironical because your objection to religion and church can be that it is of a 'bunch of conservative people closed to change or tolerance'.

'All this changes,' says Zoe Green, 'once you have experiences in your own life which defy rational explanation. The feeling of knowing you would happily die in place of your child opens an emotional connection to the idea of sacrifice which used to be purely theoretical. The experience of romantic love, against all common sense, is a mysterious force which opens an emotional connection to the sensation of faith. All of this is happening in the context of a growing awareness of mortality and life being finite. So once the feeling of faith and the search for meaning enters the picture, the idea of religion becomes much more interesting: even if you can't ever subscribe to "the rules" it still feels that there is some kind of truth lurking under the surface that religions are reaching for.'

I am drawn to this insight about immaturity and maturity. Psychologically, it can be traced backwards through the stages of childhood conceptual development, and forward through the experience of ageing when people think about their mortality and what ultimately matters, resulting in a proportion turning to religion for help. It is also true that older people may have been more exposed to religious ideas and practice in their youth and therefore have a vocabulary to engage with it. This factor of course will significantly change when the present 18–25s reach old age.

As one with a lifelong commitment to Christianity, I recognise I am biased towards religion and want to speak up for it. Organised religion in European culture seems done for, yet it has a legacy of meaning, intellectual vigour, poetry, music, community and social action which is both admirable and enticing, if only one can get to know it. It is this heritage which intensifies my puzzlement at the crevasse between the failure of organised religion in the Liberal West and the commonplace intuitive religious experience I have attempted to describe and which some prominent atheists and agnostics also speak up for. Why has spiritual imagination been separated from the Church? Is it timidity in the face of secularisation and wanting to keep hold of what little is left for fear of losing everything? Religious institutions need to live with diversity and embrace it while holding on to their core principles and seeing how those principles can adapt to changing times. I'm afraid, though, the attempts to muster diversity under the flag of 'multifaith' merely draws a few spiritual nomads and as far as I can see this does little more than provide yet another kind of small religious denomination. The ecumenical religious dialogue some argue for is elusive because most religions think they are right and often exclusively so. There is something thinly dilute about trying to find a common denominator religion and it is wearisomely unattractive.

The vigour I have experienced at firsthand in my work with young adults in this whole discourse stems to a large degree from its being contextualised in an atmosphere of enquiry in which no holds are barred and no stones unturned. This of course is the bedrock of the liberal university.

The essays which follow add to the discussion.

Notes

1   04 September 2017: The latest data on religious affiliation from NatCen's British Social Attitudes survey.

2   The figures are published in a report, Europe's Young Adults and Religion, by Stephen Bullivant, professor of theology and the sociology of religion at St Mary's University in London. They are based on data from the European social survey 2014–16.

Age of Uncertainty

By Tara Lee

I grew up in the outskirts of Hong Kong. My mother is an English woman from Worcestershire, my father, a son of Chinese immigrants who made their way to Dudley. My parents moved to my grandparents' village shortly before I was born. I was raised Catholic, and every Saturday evening my mother would drop me off at St Joseph's Church, which was built in the 1950s in a market town near the British army camp and looked vaguely European with its niches and gable roof. The church came equipped with a cheerful Italian priest who spoke a heavily accented, peculiarly musical Cantonese. My favourite bookmark was a prayer card depicting *Our Lady of China* as a cloud-treading *xian* in flowing Han dress. The hymns we sang translated Hebrew names into what sounded to me like deliciously archaic Chinese. When I took First Communion, my grandmother flew out to give me a white leather-bound missal to match my white dress (replete with frills), white shoes, and white gloves. I also went to a Catholic primary school. The prayer room, with its faded lace and vases of fresh lilies, was a cosy refuge when the playground drama became overwhelming. By contrast, the chapel in my Anglican secondary school was expensive and airy with its minimalist pale wood pews. It took me over an hour to commute to this school, which was located within the bustling Kowloon area and exposed me to an East-Asian inflection of the Protestant work ethic. These days, if I do go to Mass it is to accompany my grandma, and I go with the same attitude with which I pray to my great-grandparents with my *popo* and *gunggung*, bowing, joss-sticks in hand, to the urns holding their bones. As with many people of my generation, religion has become heritage.

I have spent some time attempting to reconstruct my path

11

to agnosticism, to pin-point the exact moment God became just another concept. Like many teenagers, I came across attacks on religion founded on logical argument, but in truth, what untied the knots of faith for me was a growing awareness of how many different blends and varieties of religion existed out there. How is Chinese folk religion any less legitimate than Christianity? The loss of certainty came with a vibrant proliferation of possibilities, but without a solid reason to choose one religion over another, faith, for me, became simply impossible. In his lecture 'The Will to Believe' (1896), the American psychologist William James speaks of hypotheses, as electricians speak of wires, as either *live* or *dead*. Ask me how my live wire died, how it was no longer an option for me to believe in a Christian God, indeed, to believe in any god or bodhisattva, any force or 'higher power' at all, and I could not point to any particular rational objection to belief, though I generally agree with these objections. Rather, it was a greater knowledge of the historical and material contingencies of religion, of the interactions between faith-systems and socio-political systems that made all these arguments fall away into irrelevance. Towards the end of my school years, I became enamoured with T. S. Eliot's poem *The Waste Land* (1922). Fascinated by the way Eliot heaped up broken images from various world religions, myths, and rituals, I turned to one of Eliot's inspirations, James Frazer's *The Golden Bough* (1890), which tried to trace different religions to their early roots as fertility cults. I began to think about religion in a new light. Religious practice appeared to me as a method of accounting for the inexplicable, a technique by which we seek to regain a sense of agency in a world that can appear alien, senseless.

The work of undoing belief never ends. Current events have prompted me to continually interrogate my beliefs and assumptions, even as these beliefs under question have become subtler, less easy to identify. In the last few years have we not all been confronted with our own hidden assumptions about the world? Have we not had to examine implicit biases around gender, for instance, and race? On an even more fundamental level, however, I understand that my ability to go about my days depends on an unspoken belief in the essential coherency of the world. I believe in cause and effect, in the unidirectional passage of time – I believe that the sun will rise tomorrow. These beliefs do their job even when we are aware that they are only beliefs.

However, magical thinking of the less pragmatic kind has managed to sneak its way back into my life every now and again. I am embarrassed to say that I have fallen in love on several occasions. One time it was with someone who had also had a conflicted relationship with Catholicism. We shared an idiom. We spoke in terms of sacrifice and love, guilt and devotion. The stakes were high. Stories scaffold romance, as they do religion. Love was a man of the desert resigning himself to a pillar of thirst. Love was lust trapped in a Dantean whirlwind. Love was a deluded missionary deep in the Amazonian region. The old tales were relevant again, briefly live. Then came the inevitable disappointment, the distress and sadness. One day I found myself passing by a Catholic church. Perhaps I thought that going into the church would make me feel briefly close to him again. A mosaic lamb looked down at me from the semi-domed ceiling of a side chapel. Underneath it two deer lapped at a fountain. Another side-chapel was spangled with stars. We go through life making and remaking our personal myths.

This is something that I have learnt from the experience. Christian faith and romantic love, as I had experienced them, both demanded a lot of emotional and mental labour. I hosted complicated debates in my inner theatre, bargaining, arguing, negotiating, wrestling with the imagined voice of an absent interlocutor. I weighed up evidence, projected motivations, constructed reasons, intuited intentions. I made space in my head for another mind, but this other mind might well have been a black box. *What does he want from me? What am I to do?* To engage in this debate is a fruitless affair. We can always find excuses on a lover's behalf. We can always construct sophistries to support a broken theology. The best strategy is to go no contact and wait for the rest of life to catch up, for old questions to grow irrelevant.

But months passed and I remained stuck. I found it difficult to wake up in the morning, difficult to drag myself to the library. My world was shrinking. My friends helped me through the worst of it. I met new people. I made progress with my thesis. Then in January rumours about a strange novel virus in China circulated in the press. By the end of March, the nation found itself placed under lockdown. The city was deserted. I was the only student left in my building. Here I was, with no company but my own, no noise but the quarter-hourly tolling of the nearby chapel bell and the sound of the voices in my head. I have always been an over-thinker. Now, stripped of all distractions, I was left with my own mind and intensifying worries about a future which seemed terribly uncertain.

It was during this time that I decided I needed to learn how to meditate. I needed to detach myself from my own thoughts, to evaluate them from a distance rather than get carried along with them. It was a deeply uncomfortable process. It took me far too long to realise that I was not supposed to control my breath. All I had to do was observe it. Slowly, I learnt to create a little space between myself and my thoughts. I read Buddhist teachings, and found much sense in the idea that our suffering comes from the attempt to fix the past and secure the future, to cling to an ever-changing world. I tried not to berate myself for every thought and feeling I could not control, an attempt which went against my Christian upbringing. I also did a lot of running. On these runs, I was occasionally surprised to find that I was visited by brief moments of – can it be? – joy.

Once, on a flight from London to Berlin, I found myself in a conversation with the friendly middle-aged Italian woman sat next to me. We talked about our experience getting to know different cities. She had truly come to feel at home in London, where – she felt like she could share this with me – she had been joining spiritual groups, beginning to explore her past lives and develop her psychic powers. 'Just my luck,' I thought, 'I'm sitting next to a fruitcake.' Then she asked me, 'Have you felt anything yourself? Have you ever been anywhere and felt a special force?' No, I thought, but then I told her that sometimes, walking along the sun-lit cliffs on the Cornish coasts, I have felt as if there were something more than was actually there. When lunch came around, she warned me to choose the veggie wrap over the chicken sandwich. 'You don't want to eat their pain. It's bad energy.'

I have asked myself about the psychology of religious experience. One Saturday afternoon, on the verge of waking up from a nap, I fell into sleep paralysis. My body felt as heavy as a glacier. Finally, after almost an hour, I managed to get out of bed. I got dressed and walked into the college gardens, with its trailing bamboo and its wisteria, hoping to shake off a sluggish sense of dread. The sun was out. Everything was beautiful. What was this presence? Each tree, each branch, seemed pregnant with insight. I could not tell you what this insight was. Try to talk about it and it comes out trite. All I could feel was a distinct feeling telling me that this moment was meaningful – a profundity without content. I tried to look into this feeling. When I was a child, one of my favourite books was an odd little book, bound in a canary yellow cover, called *Mister god, This Is Anna*. The book begins with a quotation from a little girl: 'The difference between a person and an angel is easy. Most of an angel is on the inside and most of a person is on the outside.' But is there a difference between inside and outside? When you break a rock in half, do you reveal its hidden interiors so much as to produce new surfaces? In literary studies, we have decided that all the world is a text and that the question of authorial intention is a red herring. If spirituality is focused around the occasional ineffable sense of some strange presence – well, this is something I would be glad to attribute to emergent mental phenomena rather than a creator God.

What would make any spiritual event feel genuine? My friend recently had a dissatisfactory experience with hallucinogens. For an hour he felt buoyant, happy, but ultimately it was an empty happiness, because it was a happiness without cause, a happiness without cost. There was no meaning to it. I pointed out that his five-day comedown afterwards sounded like cost enough. But there is perhaps something in what he said. Without a measure of suffering, happiness does not feel real. That is why so many of our stories are structured around success won through hardship. We find it difficult to trust the kind of happiness that comes and goes without us having to earn it.

I have another friend called Jonathan. A visiting student from Germany, Jonathan stands out in Oxford because, despite having had his own share of setbacks, he is unusually untouched by cynicism. I was talking to him once about the Christian fetishization of suffering, putting forward the idea that Christianity, as I had experienced it, invested in the idea that every mistake came with a penalty, that every indulgence had to be balanced by self-denial. He seemed confused. 'But Tara,' he said, 'I believe that everything has already been paid for.' What a beautiful idea. How I wish I could believe in it.

But I can start small. Last year, out of curiosity, I attended a Quaker Meeting in central Oxford. In the comforting silence, my eye was caught by a beam of light reflecting off the floorboards, and I was reminded of something I had read about how the seventeenth-century German mystic Jacob Boehme received one of his first visions studying an exquisite beam of sunlight reflecting off a pewter dish. A few minutes later, a parishioner stood up. He seemed to be in his 40s. Here it was, one of those moments I had been looking forward to seeing for myself, in which someone is prompted by 'that of God' inside them to arise and address the room. What he shared seemed rather more sensible than inspired. He shared his thoughts on the environmental crisis, stressing the importance of working hard on its solutions without succumbing to despair and panic. In this day and age, perhaps grounded optimism is miracle enough.

I have come to understand that, as T. S. Eliot writes, 'human kind/ Cannot bear very much reality'. To get by, some of us need to believe in a little more than the turning of the Earth and the revolution of the Sun. The head can stay as sceptical as it likes, but some of us need some stronger implicit belief to get through our days, and this belief is not something we can reason ourselves into. The paediatrician and psychoanalyst Donald Winnicott had an interesting take on this need for emotional security. According to Winnicott, the mother (or primary care giver) has an essential role in providing the baby with an adequate holding environment. She does not have to be perfect in this role, only good enough. The way she holds the infant, taking care of its every need, feeding it, bathing it, talking to it, enveloping it in her firm embrace, allows the infant to feel safe in its own body and eventually gain the courage to explore the world beyond its mother's arms. As the child ventures further out from the home to school to wider society, what keeps it strong is an internalized sense of being held and supported by this world. The child believes that the world is intact, that, however many scrapes and scratches it might acquire, all will be well, for it is loved. This is faith – a faith which is downright irrational in a world where little is secure and nothing is guaranteed.

This kind of faith eludes me. Would it be more useful for sceptical people like me to think in term of values instead of faith? I value beauty. I value kindness. I value wisdom. And I know that I will find beauty and kindness and wisdom in people wherever I go. Perhaps not a lot – but I have found so much of it already, in friends and strangers, even when I had lost faith in the world. If I cannot believe that the world is whole, I can at least believe that the world contains fragments of what is good. And what if things work out? Perhaps, to borrow the words of Geoffrey Hill, 'This is plenty. This is more than enough.'

An Altered Default and Apathy to Faith

By Christopher T. Bennett

Winston Churchill allegedly said that 'the best argument against democracy is a five-minute conversation with the average voter.' The more uncharitable (or condescending) observer might say the same of atheism or theism. As one who has studied the philosophy of religion for a number of years academically, I often find conversation with other young people about faith frustrating. Yet this is as much my fault as theirs – many simply do not assign religion great importance in their psyche. It may have played a key role in my life but it often barely figures for others, and their reasons behind their positions are typically weak or non-existent. It is the minority who have considered the matter at length before coming to a conclusion. My interests do not necessarily make me more enlightened or correct than those who don't study religion, it simply means that we have different things that we spend our time pondering. Nonetheless, the disparity bears further investigation, particularly for those for whom religion is something that *should* be extensively pondered.

Here I offer the insights that come from being a theologically trained person who frequently discusses religious matters with young people from various faith backgrounds. Particularly because I am approaching this subject from a fairly secular but sympathetic perspective, what I will say should be both absorbing and helpful in pointing towards profitable avenues for religious leaders. These will be my honest thoughts and feelings on modern faith, interpreting how my friends and acquaintances in the UK approach belief. Without understanding how young people truly feel and think about religion, its very future might be in jeopardy. My qualitative impression is that the way my generation approaches religion is largely no different from previous generations. This does not, however, necessarily sound a hopeful note for promoters of faith in modern society.

Introduction

I'm very much culturally Christian, having attended a Catholic school where I participated in Mass every week and engaged with religious music in choirs. My mother is religious and was keen to ensure that I followed her in that (though she was never pushy) so we went to church occasionally throughout my childhood and I was confirmed in the Church of England as a teenager. In my latter years of schooling, and during my undergraduate degree, I engaged less and less with religion, partly because of changing beliefs but primarily due to the pressures of work and leaving the explicitly religious environment of my school. Moving to the present, every year I attend church at Easter and Christmas, but rarely outside those two occasions. It would definitely be an exaggeration to say that I am actively religious nowadays. Hence, I reside firmly in a grey area between religion and atheism, and am definitely not a strong Christian believer, without being a fervent secularist either.

My religious beliefs are further complicated by my study of Theology at a postgraduate level; I have undergone significant academic study of religion. I find religion thoroughly fascinating: historically, psychologically and philosophically. Seeking to understand religion, in all its many forms, need not lead to belief in it though. While my academic study of religion definitely did not push me away or towards faith, it distanced me intellectually. I typically consider myself philosophically agnostic on the question of God's existence, largely because I find that this helps me to approach my studies objectively. My work involves investigating and assessing the success of arguments for and against God's existence. Indeed, when working I might find myself attacking a theist's proposal, then in the next breath criticising the atheistic counter too. It is of course impossible to approach such matters from an unbiased position, but by engaging with a variety of opinions across the spectrum, I at least aim to give all credible options equal weighting until I have fully examined their merits. This means that my academic experience of religion inclines me towards a sort of 'disinterested researcher' stance.

My background informs my opinions on religion, as it does for everyone. The fact that I was raised Anglican meant that I had natural affinity to that denomination, despite my Catholic schooling, though I was often confused as a child by the ostensibly tiny (but theologically vast) differences in liturgy between the two. Engaging in musical events at my Catholic school gave me positive associations with faith, as I always enjoyed singing praises to God, regardless of the fact that I rarely had any idea that I was doing so! On the other hand, being immersed in a University culture for several years where religious belief is not normal undeniably drew me away from strong belief. It also perhaps nudged me in the direction of seeing religion as something that is not personal to me, as many other contributors to this volume view it, but instead is a subject for examination and analysis.

What does all this mean? I would highlight the caveat that I do not think my own personal background is incredibly fascinating. Much of what I have said so far applies to many other people up and down this country. My lack of uniqueness can be as much a strength as it is a weakness though, because my views originate from a common outlook. Another salient point stemming from my background is that I feel qualified to discuss a variety of religious points with a spectrum of believers. I also like to approach religion from an external, essentially agnostic position. These two facts in tandem have permitted me to gather a range of the views that are common among other young people. I do not claim to be an impartial, perfect transmitter of views. Still, certain elements of my life leave me well qualified to offer novel insights into the attitudes of my peers on religious matters. I offer qualitative information on British society that explains the large numbers of our youth that have 'no religion' far more deeply and holistically than a simple survey can convey.

Attitudes Towards Religion

In conversation with friends and acquaintances, a naturally common topic of conversation is what I'm doing with my life. Aside from the typical 'nothing productive' answer, I tell them that I fill my days pondering the philosophy of religion (meaning I really just give one answer with different wordings). The common assumption, upon discovering this bizarre propensity, is that I must therefore be intensely religious, mad, or both. Indeed, perhaps half of people to whom I speak require multiple assurances that I'm not aiming to be a priest, and that I'm certainly not trying to convert them! People find it not only perplexing that I study religion from a secular perspective, but genuinely conceptually difficult. They cannot really understand why anyone would be passionate enough to study religion, unless they were personally participating.

Why is this so? Of course, cultural issues are at play here. Many people see degrees as vocational, aiming towards a job, so struggle to understand the study of something for pure academic interest. But there is more to it than that. I think many people don't understand my reasoning for doing theology because religion is not a big feature in their lives. If faith is not a subject that one considers every day, then one is naturally going to be puzzled by the study of it. Hence, my study of religion might look as odd to them as the study of Geoffrey Chaucer's writings look to me, a person with very little mediaeval literary interest. Coupled with this is the notion that unless I am a Christian, I couldn't possibly be interested in studying Christianity. To an outsider, it might be like saying 'I find Chaucer's works to be dull and uninspired, yet have dedicated the last decade of my life to the study of them.' When you add the lack of interest in religion itself to the notion that there is little point in studying something unless one believes it to be particularly powerful, true or useful, I think you begin to understand why my study of theology seems so peculiar to so many.

The reactions of curiosity reveal much about religion among the youth of today. I should add that both believers and non-believers typically respond with similar surprise. Naturally, I can believe that religion is an incredibly important and influential topic of study without believing it to be entirely true. In some ways, what I do is similar to scientific study, as I aim to test religious propositions. Science is far more than a matter of confirming truths as they immediately appear; likewise, theology is a rigorous discipline, not passive acceptance at all. I am not aiming to defend the value of theology as an academic subject, merely seeking to understand why other young people in particular find my study of it so peculiar. Often, when I state that I study the philosophy of religion as opposed to scripture, comprehension seems to dawn. Yet surely even a person who disagrees with every word of the Bible could study it? One conclusion I draw from this theme is that others of my generation do not, at first, understand the academic side to religion. More significantly, I also infer that the notion of religion's significance to society, and hence any value to be found in studying it, has been relegated to an oddity due to its unpopularity. Although it is not impossible to explain to most interlocutors why I do study theology, that default curiosity is intriguing.

The 'default mode' is a motif to which I will return on a number of occasions, as I believe it is illuminating when considering young people's religion. The next step in conversation, after explaining what I do and why, will usually take the form of my asking what my conversation partner's faith is. I do not wish to rely upon my anecdotal evidence alone here, so will refer to the most recent census, in 2011. In that year, just 25% of respondents aged 0–24 stated that they were Christian. Now, considering the circles in which I move are typically filled with higher-educated, wealthier people, and adjusting for the eight years since the census was carried out, I would say of the proportions of people to whom I speak 25% is an overstatement. Indeed, grouping 'all religions' together might lead to a result of 25%, but I am struck by the fact that the overwhelming majority of my contacts openly describe themselves in that non-descript category of 'non-religious'. This accords with recent research discussed elsewhere that suggests circa 70% of 16–29-year-olds are non-religious. Hence, my experiences are at least somewhat representative when they suggest that young people are, by and large, not a religious set of the population at large.

This much is obvious and not new, though the quantitative data is startling and unsettling (depending on your viewpoint). By relating the most frequent kinds of discussion I have on the matter, I will offer a holistic story behind that data, reflecting the common rationales and sentiments undergirding the lack of religious feeling in young people. In that effort, I will begin by discussing some of the key reasons that lead young people to be non-religious. In my conversations with peers, I often find myself taking on the sort of impromptu role of 'secular defender of faith' – especially when met with unfair caricatures of religious positions. Given my own far from fervent religious proclivities, it is funny to imagine that I might have rehabilitated many people's opinions of Christianity (and other faiths). In fact, I daresay I've swung more people to a favourable opinion by gentle nudging and recharacterisation than any street preacher shouting at passers-by (perhaps not a high bar)!

Why Believe?
Possibly the most commonly expressed reason when I ask why a person does not believe in God is 'why should I?'. Without

tediously expounding the opus of Aquinas, Descartes or other genius, but perhaps removed from the modern setting, thinkers, it is not easy to give a succinct answer. Anyway, my 'secular defender of the faith' role does not stretch to persuading others philosophically. Convincing cultural reasons for belief have vanished. Whereas once upon a time every young person might have been constantly exposed to religious arguments and emotion, nowadays it is perfectly possible to live a totally fulfilled life without ever being presented with reason to believe. Regardless of the strength of the reasoning one might have been exposed to in the past, one would at least have been aware of natural theology, that some people would aim to persuade you of God's existence. Nowadays, it seems that has all but disappeared, meaning young people see no reason to believe.

Needless to say, my idealistic philosophical standpoint may be entirely inappropriate for this area – indeed the last half a decade has probably taught us that rational argument often plays a minor role in the population's belief systems. But most people, both in the past and in the present, form their beliefs based on their cultural context. It is also interesting that the cultural context has shifted more than the permeation of philosophical theology. I would wager in the past that speaking to many young people about why they are Christian might earn me the common response 'why shouldn't I be?'. They would likely say this for many of the same reasons that the secular youth of today say the opposite. The fact that religion no longer pervades culture not only means people are unaware of the rich theological landscape, but also alters their default position from one of Christianity to one of 'no religion'.

Now, this 'unthinking' response is far from the only response. Critical thinking does exist in today's young people! If I am given a reason for why they don't believe, people often tell me about how much suffering there is in the world, or how God's presence is hardly obvious. The philosopher within me recognises the problems of Evil and Divine Hiddenness rearing their heads. If nothing else, it is gratifying to know that real life people care about these issues, not only obsessed academics... Still, I should not over-emphasise the impression that religious beliefs have been carefully considered, arguments weighed and a rational decision made. Even among those I talk to who have clearly given some thought to the matter, there isn't much awareness of other points of view, or a real willingness to challenge one's own suppositions. I have spoken to *some* believers and non-believers who are aware of the broader theological literature, attempted to engage with it, then made their decision on that basis. But they are a tiny minority, dwarfed by those who have little or no basis for their beliefs, and do not understand how things could be otherwise.

I would like to make plain again that I am not trying to be an intellectual snob. I am not arguing that every person, or every young person, ought to be familiar with any part of philosophy of religion before they are permitted to opine on religious affairs. That way madness lies. The lack of interest in engaging in any great depth with what to many are fundamentally important issues is intriguing though. It exemplifies the decreased importance of religion in the psyche of young people that most of my acquaintances do not trouble themselves with rational consideration of its potential truth, despite being intelligent, thoughtful people themselves. Many engage with complex arguments in the fields of politics, science or the arts, but express no interest in doing so on religion. Some are aware of the complexity of the matter and simply wish not to get involved, perhaps because it is such an emotive and labyrinthine affair. In any case, I think the lack of strong reasoning behind religious opinions in young people is most indicative of religion's fading significance in the modern world, rather than pig-headed anti-theological arrogance.

Unfortunately, there are some young people I have discussed

religion with who present me with poor reasoning that doesn't stand up to even casual enquiry. In such cases, I struggle to remain charitable, because the arguments I encounter are often so plainly ridiculous that gentle prodding alone causes the crumbling of the edifice. For example, some interlocutors raise the example of creationism, as part of an argument that religion is 'anti-science'. This not only plays into the discredited narrative of conflict between the two fields of enquiry, but is also a very poor reason not to believe, because there are plenty of religious scientists and comparatively few creationists. When I point out examples of scientific discoveries that were made by monks, priests, etc., I am often told that in those cases the science being done was separate from the religious impulses. True or not, it is inconsistent that only when there is a positive relationship between science and religion can we not look at individual examples, whereas atheists are happy to consider the minority of fervently anti-science Christians and tar all believers with the same brush.

I credit ignorance of religious doctrine, and its implications, to the pernicious excesses of New Atheism. The movement likely formed a major part of most of my generation's first experiences of philosophy. Certainly, I watched YouTube and Facebook clips throughout my teenage years of Richard Dawkins, Daniel Dennett and other classic New Atheists discussing religion in a derogatory way, and found myself agreeing purely because of the incomplete and contextless way in which such ideas are presented. It is hard to expect a high level of religious literacy from anyone whose information is based on little more than 5-minute, non-representative fragments of theological views that have either been dumbed-down or cherry picked for their stupidity. Hence, the best explanation for the fact that some young people seem to have irrational, strongly anti-religious views is that they have been misled, and similarly to the 'unthinking' atheists, do not care to investigate further.

Although from the outside such people may seem to be hostile religion-haters, a far better explanation is apathy. There are also far fewer of these actively anti-theistic young people than is often feared.

Apathy has been a recurring theme in my conversations and thus in my piece so far. One of the feelings that transmits to me most strongly when I attempt to probe into my acquaintances' religious beliefs, or even attempt to engage them in theological discussion, is a sense that there is little point discussing or worrying about religion. This idea pops up when considering my own field of study, when being given little reason for someone's religious beliefs, or even when being told that religion is wrong. At an extreme, I have been told that no one could ever possibly know whether Christianity is true, so what difference does it make? That is a sort of justification for apathy, but not a common one, in my experience. Most, when pushed, do appreciate that there probably is a fact of the matter out there, and humans can probably have a good stab at learning what it is. Nonetheless, when approaching the topic, genuine indifference towards religious matters is what strikes me most frequently. This seeps into rationality too, because all people are unlikely to delve deeply into the minutiae of philosophical argument on a matter for which they see little real-world importance. Hence, young people in particular, if they do not believe that religiosity is a relevant factor for them and society at large, are likely to retain their stance of being non-religious without trouble.

Having set out my thesis on the power and prevalence of apathy, it would be wrong to take it as a point of difference between my and other generations. I fervently want to avoid the impression that young, non-religious people are stupider or less interested in the world than previous generations, and that *that* is the cause of decline in religiosity. Apathy leading to non-belief is just a symptom of the much larger variable that has changed between this generation and earlier generations.

The critical alteration is the transformation of default. I speak here of the culture at large rather than specific people. I am no cultural anthropologist, and I do not wish to downplay the Christian legacy that permeates modern British society, but it seems evident that Christianity, and religion in general, is a far less influential cultural force now, as opposed to even just thirty years ago.

At some point over the last century the lack of religious influence in society reduced below its critical mass. The numbers have decreased steadily over that time, which quickly becomes a self-fulfilling downward spiral. Critical mass is a term originating in nuclear physics, denoting the mass of radioactive material required for the chain reaction of nuclear fission to continue unaided. Co-opted by sociological circles, it began to mean the number of people required to be involved in an activity for its continuation and growth to be self-sustaining. I do not pretend to know what the critical mass of a religion is (though that seems to me a very interesting question). Yet I feel confident in stating that most religions in the UK are firmly below that threshold nationwide (in certain localities there may be pockets of self-sustaining faith communities).

Not achieving critical mass means that the 'chain reaction' of religion passing from person to person has stopped in contemporary British society. In my opinion, this is the most significant factor in religion's decay. Far be it from me to say why the decline began or persisted, but once the percentage of the population who were religious dipped below critical mass, a reverse snowball effect ensures that the decline will continue. Children are no longer taught to pray, nor attend church with their parents; schools cease teaching Christianity with especial attention due to its dominant cultural position, people stop encountering religious ideas in everyday situations. It is clear to see how a lack of religion gradually escalates and causes exponential decline. People of my generation are at the vanguard of the chain reaction's conclusion. Hence, many will not understand casual biblical references in normal conversation (much to the chagrin of my friends I do occasionally refer to parables or quote psalms, which would have been far more commonly understood memes a couple of generations ago), or give religion due consideration on a day-to-day basis. This is perhaps the apotheosis of a society of 'no religion' – religious belief cannot re-establish itself due to its very unpopularity.

A New Default

So far, I hope I have demonstrated that, on the basis of conversations I have had, young people largely feel apathy towards religion, do not consider it in their normal lives, and that this has come about largely because of the loss of a critical mass of religious believers. Together, these factors lie behind the prevalence of 'no religion' in Britain today. The other impact of the loss of critical mass is the change in default, that I have already mentioned on a number of occasions and on which I will now focus more attention. The default has changed not just in the broader culture but also at the more particular, personal level. Young people whose default beliefs fifty years ago might have been religious are now much more likely to be by default non-religious. A girl who in bygone years might have attended Sunday school and then church throughout her childhood because her parents took her and that was just the way things were might nowadays visit churches on holiday and otherwise barely set foot inside one. Likewise, fifty years ago there would have been very few people who would not have either had religious parents, or gone to a religious school, or been surrounded by religious friends. One's environment is a tremendous influence on one's beliefs. Hence, the change in environment brought about by the loss of religious critical mass can be directly attributed as the key cause of the change in default.

Given that not only has society's default religion changed, but each individual now is overwhelmingly more likely to be initially atheist or agnostic, there are major implications for how we conceptualise and respond to faltering religiosity. For one thing, it is important to recognise the impersonal nature of the change. The switch in default religion across the whole of society cannot be laid at the feet of any one person or factor, and even its consequences at a personal level are largely out of the control of the individual person. When I talk to an agnostic friend who has never sat in a single church service, I can hardly accuse them of carelessness or ignorance for not considering Christianity. A person who has never encountered religion has no chance or inclination whatsoever to join one. When the default has switched, people experience a completely different set of life circumstances from before. Considering the sheer breadth of human experience, it is hardly surprising that many do not give religion much thought as a result.

So the change in default can partially explain the growth in apathy, as well as atheism. However, as I alluded to before, I do not think that the most significant change in recent times is an increase in apathy towards consideration of religious matters. Indeed, in terms of deep reflection and introspection on theology, I doubt that apathy is really any more present in young people today than it is in any other generation at any other time period (I doubt medieval churchgoers who did not even understand the language of their services had philosophical defences of their faith). Here is where the change in default rises again as the ultimately important factor. Peers struggle to understand why I would bother, as someone fairly secular, to study theology because being religious is no longer the *normal* or default position. They do not see the value in devoting one's life to something that is neither what one believes in nor part of modern-day dominant social narratives.

To highlight further the primacy of the default switch as an explanatory factor, I recall similar conversations with people of older generations. There's a smaller sample size but still noticeable trends. The differences, beyond religious inclination, are largely superficial. From a philosophical standpoint, I am just as likely to receive a poorly reasoned answer to an inquiry into the grounds of a believer's faith as a non-believer's lack thereof. Moreover, acquaintances from other generations do not consistently provide any reasons for their religious beliefs. Similarly, to the answer I discussed above where an atheist asks me 'why should' she be religious, a believer very commonly asks 'why shouldn't' she be religious. Of course, I have no useful answer to give them, because neither has really thought it was a decision that required justification. The lack of rational enquiry into theological positions, I venture, is not new at all. What is new is that where once someone who paid religion no mind would instinctively believe, a young person who gives religion no consideration instinctively does not believe. The change in the default position completely alters the framework in which young people operate, so there has been no seismic shift in critical thinking skills or attention paid to philosophy of religion, merely a difference in default beliefs that brings with it significant aftershocks.

Of course, I am generalising to a great extent here, as there are numerous people of all ages whose religious inclinations are, if not wholly rational, then at least somewhat based in reasonable reflection. Not everyone is a cultural sponge, soaking up whatever religious sentiment happens to pervade his surroundings. I do not wish to discount or downplay the influence this has on religiosity. Nevertheless, recall some examples that I spelt out above even of people who do rationalise their theological views. Among those who provide me with arguments behind their opinions, such views are often ill-conceived, and almost always ignorant of the broader context in which they sit. Hence, in practice I can count on one hand the number of people I have met who tell me they have substantively changed their religion since adulthood. This is perhaps indicative of the emotive, non-rational status of religious beliefs, but it is also a common feature across generations. Therefore, taking all of what I have said together, I am convinced that the differentiating factor for young people today causing the growth of 'no religion' is their default, unconscious attitudes, not so much their conscious, discerning positions.

Implications

My hypothesis that a largely impersonal change is responsible for the decline in religiosity in modern British society, especially among young people, has a number of consequences. Uppermost among them is that one ought to desist from being scathing about young people, as can be tempting. Some of the discussions I encounter and have described are fairly appalling from a rigorously rational perspective, and would seem to paint a picture of 'stupid youths not thinking straight'. Churchill's alleged observation can seem to be sagely apt for religion. Yet I disagree that this generation is any less capable of rational thought than any other; in fact, I would like to believe we are even more so. It is merely the case that no significant portion of any generation has devoted a major part of its thinking to religious enquiry. People are busy and have other (and, some would *foolishly* claim, better) things to do. Where one might have once gone to church somewhat unthinkingly, because it was tradition, now one just as unthinkingly does not go to church.

If indeed I am correct, there are obvious implications for Christians who wish to ensure that society remains religious and young people are not excluded from their religion. The main implication is negative – due to the impersonal nature of the change, and the somewhat intangible character of the 'default', I can suggest no easy way to reverse Christianity's decline. It seems that the currents of society have moved and continue to move such that religion is swept away in all but the more dedicated pockets. How to alter the mood of a society? It is a question for which I have no answer, and I do not relish attempting to find one. Schools decreasingly teach religion in detail; media and culture are decreasingly shot through with Christianity, and the public are less inclined to discuss religion as a serious system of thought. To add to this, life is incredibly busy, with one million and one possible occupations competing for the attention of every young person. Even if they are interested in or disposed towards religion, they are much less likely to dedicate time to it. Altogether, these factors have formed a toxic brew that makes approaching young people in an effort to encourage religiosity nigh on impossible, possibly even counter-productive. Traditional Evangelism surely is not the answer.

Despite the doom and gloom of my last paragraph, some chinks of light in the cloudy forecast I present may exist. For one, it is hopefully comforting to hear that in many ways things are the same as they ever were. It would be on the whole more worrying, I think, if there had been some rational or pseudo-rational rebellion against religion. I mentioned Dawkins, Dennett and other New Atheists (decide for yourself where these fall on the rational to pseudo-rational spectrum) but it is rarely the case that young people have spent large periods of time weighing and considering different arguments for and against religion before deciding. Remember the power of the default. Nor, equally, do most young people to whom I spoke have an especially negative opinion towards religion. Rather, they simply do not think of it at all. Apathy is better than Antipathy. On the whole then, I believe this means that the reasons to be cheerful boil down pretty similarly to the reasons to be fearful. The path for religion to reassert itself seems clear – it must somehow regain its place as the default societal strain of thought. The fearful part of that is just how difficult a task that is, and how uncertain the road towards it looks.

Although I have been focussed in this chapter primarily on what non-religious young people think and say, it would be remiss of me not to survey briefly the thoughts I receive from religious acquaintances. My outsider's perspective on these matters is hopefully more refreshing than limiting, seeing as it bears relevance for the broader response to irreligiosity. The religious young people to whom I speak are typically quite devoted. Unlike many of the young atheists and agnostics, for whom that part of their lives plays almost no role, religious young people are much keener to discuss the centrality of their faith to them. They will often be regular attendees at church, participate in the Christian community of their church or University, and bring up their faith casually in conversation. The proportion of young people who are just barely religious, or describe themselves as Christian despite not really thinking about God, is tiny. Again, this is not to say that all such acquaintances have reached their faith positions based on strong evidence and are much better theologically informed than their secular counterparts (often they are no better able to defend their views than the apathetic atheists discussed earlier), merely that their faith is very significant in their lives.

This is a stark contrast from non-religious young people, and one that can again be attributed to the change in default. In general, the most important parts of one's psyche are not those areas that are most commonly held. I have two arms and two legs, yet those aren't major things central to being 'me'. Instead, more niche elements such as my birthplace, or my interests in Kanye West, Ultimate Frisbee and dystopian fiction, or my support for Newcastle United (for my sins) become more identifiably key facets of 'me'. As more unique elements of my identity, I naturally devote more time to them. Similarly, due to the change in default, being religious is now a minority position, and very much so among young people. This means that what might once have been an uninteresting feature has become a defining, central characteristic of one's ego, because it now differentiates one from the rest of the crowd. Accordingly, one is more likely to engage with it more wholeheartedly.

In addition to this factor, there is also a level of selection bias creeping in here. In order for one to *stay* religious within a society where the prevailing, default mood has become secular, one must be pretty jolly religious. Hence, the only young people who are likely to be religious nowadays are those who were initially inclined very strongly towards religion, as those with a weaker inclination might have been dissuaded by the general mood. Naturally, all these implications and inferences from my conversations are speculation. Buried within the speculations, though, is potentially valuable insight into why the few religious young people there are are strongly religious, and why it might thus not be a good idea to look to this minority as representative of the population at large. There seem therefore to be few useful lessons to learn from religious youths – one must instead consider why 'no religion' has become so prevalent, in order to understand the attitudes of today's young people.

Morality and Substitutes

Having given my melancholy projection on the future of religion, I want to look briefly at some related issues. For one, where does this discussion leave morality? For hundreds of years, ethics were intertwined with religious sentiment, to which the Bishops in the House of Lords and the Bibles in the courtrooms pay testament. The historical legacy of Christian ethics has not, in my view, yet been expunged from society's moral undercurrent but modern Christianity holds little explicit moral or legal sway. Given the change of default that I have discussed to non-religion, this seemingly leaves us either with the option of losing our moral compass as we lose our religion, or detaching morality from religion somehow. The former notion is a popular one in some quarters, and perhaps understandably so, given the often shocking examples of immorality (or amorality) in modern-day society, which leave some questioning whether ethics is dying with religion.

I contest this rather cynical line of thinking. It is easy to look towards the past and imagine that things were better then. But today's young people, irreligious though they may largely be, are not devoid of moral sentiment. There is a strong willingness to fight for equal rights against perceived and real injustices that afflict minorities. There is a truly globalist outlook that, more than ever before, makes young people see themselves as 'citizens of the world'. Tied in with this, young people feel passionately about the climate disaster being inflicted upon our planet. A critic might point out that young people have made very little progress in these areas, beyond petitions and nice words, but this is hardly different from any other generations when dealing with such widespread issues. I am not stating definitively that on any of these issues the young people are morally in the right, fighting against the world's wrongs. However, these are blatant examples that my generation has not forgotten its ethical impulses in the way it has forgotten religion, though the values themselves may change between generations.

Indeed, returning to some sample conversations I have had with other young people about religion, the theme of ethics often crops up. Those who are even a little informed about Christianity will often express the view that while of course God could not possibly exist, and the whole thing must be a fabrication, that doesn't change the fact that Jesus was a very kind man indeed. The common refrain 'Jesus and the Buddha are just great teachers, after all, aren't they?' can be heard again and again on this topic. Some might find such a speculation theologically offensive. Indeed, I occasionally aim to persuade my interlocutors that perhaps each man wanted his legacy to be a little more than that. Nevertheless, there is evidently a recognition implicit in such a statement that ethics is an important part of religion and life. Moreover, the ethics begin to detach from the overarching metaphysics, so that we might treat Jesus as an ethical theorist in the same way that we treat Immanuel Kant or John Stuart Mill, perhaps. Whether this is a positive or negative thing, I leave up to the reader. But I see it as convincing evidence that religion and ethics are viewed as separate entities, and the latter can exist apart from the former.

Another interesting question that often arises is – what has replaced religion? This question stems either from an assumption that the change in default leaves a vacuum in the lives of young people, or from the theory that religion has been pushed out by some other phenomenon. I do not have much truck with either view. The first I think misunderstands how young people conceptualise religion, and the second I take to be wrong in its ultimate diagnosis of religion's decline. Young people might have many problems facing them in modern society, but I don't think a lack of religion is one that afflicts them particularly. Those non-religious young people to whom I have spoken certainly don't feel as if their life has a religion-shaped hole, and the implication of such a notion is that religion fills a somewhat unique niche in the human psyche. But much of what I have said has been to the effect that religious belief is now just a worldview among worldviews, so there is no niche and thus no vacuum left by its absence. In terms of the theory that religion was 'pushed out' by some other phenomenon, it ought to be plain from what I have said before that I don't think any such active removal or replacement caused religion's decline, aside of course from a general secular sentiment, to which I think it would be wrong to attribute too much agency.

Nonetheless, one interesting way to investigate the possibility of religion being pushed out is by considering how plausible potential 'replacement' candidates for religion are. A common option is 'science'. Hand-in-hand with this comes 'capitalism'. The two in tandem are commonly conceived as standard-bearers for a materialistic, post-Christianity world, which expresses itself in our investigations of the world through Science and in our interactions with each other through capitalism. Having discussed this possibility with acquaintances, I don't believe that either has really replaced religion. It seems tempting to say so, as science now is often looked towards as the ultimate explainer of the world and source of hope for the future. Likewise, capitalism, in the form of material goods, seems to provide goals and aspirations and even hierarchy, dependent on fulfilling these goals. All of these features resemble key roles played by religion in the past.

Certainly, some elements of religion can be found in non-religious pursuits. Yet science lacks transcendent, supernatural elements, as does materialistic capitalism, meaning neither is as all-encompassing a worldview as religion once was. Furthermore, speaking to young people gives me the impression that while certain parts of religious life might have been replaced, they don't treat science in a religious way, insofar as there is no deep, unshakeable faith or community with which to join. Science is accepted as fallible, and though people certainly appreciate its insights, it does not typically provide them with a sense of belonging or something over which to obsess. Hence, I do not think that 'science' (or a materialism more broadly, including capitalism) is a worthy candidate for replacing religion. The fact that these weighty areas of human pursuit do not constitute replacements of religion demonstrates further the enormity of religion's role in society, and what has seemingly disappeared.

Another common replacement candidate for religion is 'spiritualism', by which I mean the idea that 'traditional' religions in the West are being replaced by rituals often tangentially related to Paganism or Eastern religions, whether this comes in the form of nature-worship, healing power crystals, or trying to get in touch with one's inner self through Yoga or Tai Chi, as just a few myriad examples. It is true that many of these practices have grown as Christianity's prevalence has waned. They do fill a similar niche in the human psyche as Christianity did. However, when I speak to other young people it is fairly rare for them to think of themselves as being 'spiritual'. While they might do yoga, or obsess over their star signs, or even (rarely) engage in druid-like practices, these are seen first and foremost as cultural events that serve a functional purpose. Though many of these various, growing practices seem to aim towards the supernatural realm, they are not perceived in a religious way by many of their practitioners. There is no doctrine, no formal beliefs, little community. Of course, a strict definition is impossible, and certainly some aspects of these practices are fulfilling similar roles to religion. My overarching comment here, though, is that not very many young people actually engage in such practices, and many of those who do, do so because of the functional benefit or sheer fun, rather than buying into a metaphysical system.

Conclusion

To conclude, this chapter has provided the perspective of a so-called 'secular defender of the faith', engaging with possible theories for religion's decline within the context of conversations with other young people. By adding qualitative impressions to the growing, overwhelming data on the growth of the 'non-religious', a thicker description of the phenomenon can be achieved. Apathy towards religion was one major common theme to emerge from these conversations, a mood that is best explained by the significant cultural shift British society has experienced in recent years towards no religion. Another major trend was the seeming irrationality of religious beliefs, from both theists and atheists to whom I spoke, wherein justification was often weak or absent. Both of these strands can be tied together, I suggested, by comprehending the importance of a change in the default religious atmosphere. In contemporary British culture people are by default non-religious, where only a couple of generations ago they would have been by default religious. The vast majority of people's religious preferences are dictated by their default views. Hence, evidence of irrationality or apathy of religion must be understood within the context of an altered default, meaning that the major difference between my generation and others is impersonal, and the rise of 'no religion' is self-fulfilling. Sorry, but the bad news is accompanied by more bad news.

The ultimate meanings of this change in default are various. The major implication of the impersonality of the change means that it will not be easy for Christians to win back their flocks. They must somehow inspire a change in the broader societal conception of religion, with the aim of swinging the default back in their favour. My conversations with other young people suggest that trying to win over individuals is likely to be ineffective, or even counter-productive. As for how one might go about resetting society's default religion though, I can offer no help. Another observed effect of the different default is that morality has separated from religion, so still exists for young people but in a much more secular setting. Moreover, my theory precludes the need for any 'replacement' theory of religion being supplanted by another phenomenon. My conversations with young people have made clear to me that there are no easy ways forward for those who wish to promote faith, and that is the final element of gloom I have to offer religious leaders. The impersonal, default nature of the change means that understanding and patience must be shown when discussing such matters with members of my generation, resisting the frustration that Churchill allegedly felt when talking to his voters. Only by gradually restarting the chain reaction of religious community in British society will young people eventually turn away from 'no religion'.

Faith, Science and Certainty

By Ben Winchester

Richard Holloway, the contemporary writer and former Bishop of Edinburgh, has argued that the opposite of faith is not doubt, but certainty. I am interested to see whether certainty is the root cause of the widely perceived rift between science and religion. What is certainty? Can we be certain of anything? Should we be? And where does belief fit into this?

I went to a Church of England primary school in a small rural village. After my first day of school, I came home and told my parents 'we had a christening today.' The next day I informed them 'we had another christening today.' I thought that our daily school assemblies, which, in reality, featured Christian prayer, were christenings as these had been my only experience of any kind of church so far, and that during them we prayed not to God, but to the headmaster.

My next school could not have been more different. Whereas my primary school had been lifted out of Victorian England (I once dislocated my thumb while rubbing out some work because the teacher wouldn't give me an eraser), my secondary school was an exemplary modern comprehensive. We were taught in concrete blocks that had sliding glass windows. I was told there was no God, at any level, in the universe; that life on Earth, and the Big Bang, were random, chance events; and that there could be nothing beyond all that we see.

Nowadays, I'd say I'm a semi-Christian, nature-loving agnostic: a mash-up of the Christianity embedded deep within me by those daily assemblies, an appreciation of our natural world discovered by wandering through fields and skimming stones across the Wye as a teenager, and the seeds of questioning sown by a scientific education.

Having arrived somewhere between religion and science, I

find myself surrounded by supporters deeply entrenched on one side or the other, people who have dug themselves in so firmly they have left themselves little room to move. Are science and religion really two separate camps, two sides squaring up across no man's land, or can the two be reconciled? I remember a Biology lesson where our teacher lambasted 'the theory of intelligent design' as passionately as any minister would preach the gospel. While there is more archaeological and biological evidence for one than the other, are they mutually exclusive? Are these two different educational poles that I experienced so far apart, or can they be brought together?

I'll look briefly at the creation story, and delve a little into what we know about the origins of the Universe.

Light travels at 300 million metres per second, or around 670 million miles per hour. This means that, the farther away a star is, the longer it has taken for its light to reach us, and so, when we look up at the night sky, we're really seeing stars and galaxies as they used to be, ten, a hundred, or a billion years ago. The night sky is a window into the past.

To look back in time, therefore, we need only look up and out into space. There is a limit, however, to how far back in time we can look with our telescopes. Not to the beginning of time, but the beginning of light, or, rather, of 'free light'. In the early universe, the electrons and protons which make up matter existed separately. Photons could only travel a short distance before hitting some matter and being caught and spat out again on some new tack. The universe was opaque. Then suddenly the hot mix cooled enough to allow hydrogen, the lightest of the elements, to form. Photons could now travel freely in all directions.

Under the slow force of gravity, and on vast cosmic timescales, scattered atoms and dust came together to form nebulae: clouds in space where stars are born. This process of gradual accretion and gaining mass continued over billions of years, and is still going on today, with these star-forming clouds gaining dust and matter until they eventually become dense enough to ignite and form stars. Any one star may live for tens of billions of years.

At the end of its life, if large enough, a star may violently explode, scattering its remnants across the cosmos. The immense heat and pressure in these explosions, called supernovae, is thought to be responsible for the formation of all the heavy elements. (These are those elements heavier than Iron.) The iron in our blood, the calcium in our bones, and the potassium in our skin are all made from long-dead stars. I find it humbling to think that these stars are still burning within us, that we are their legacies and their life still flows through our veins. Remembering the enormity of our universe and the vastness of time really puts our daily troubles into perspective.

In our Universe, this cycle of stellar birth, life, and death repeats itself. This process ran for over eight billion years until the right mixture of elements built up to form our solar system as we know it. At the beginning of our solar system, our star began its life surrounded by a disc of dust, comets, and asteroids, which, over roughly one hundred thousand years, coalesced, through many collisions, to form larger and larger bodies. We call eight of these the planets.

The moon has a very similar chemical composition to the Earth. Scientists think that a large collision between the Earth and another body occurred when the Earth was still forming, knocking off a great chunk of material from our planet. This piece of hot, molten material is thought to have cooled to form our moon.

Our Earth began its life hot and molten and gradually cooled over millions of years. Icy comets from the outer solar system are thought to have brought water, and perhaps bacterial life, to our dry and dusty world, and eventually filled the canyons and ravines with water to form the lakes and seas.

We wouldn't have been able to breathe our early atmosphere.

It contained very little oxygen and toxic levels of carbon dioxide, a gas whose greenhouse-warming powers have driven runaway Global Warming on the planet Venus, and whose effects are likely to be felt more and more as the consequences of Global Warming here on Earth begin to take hold. Despite being inhospitable to us, this deadly air provided the perfect environment for photosynthesis and for plants. As the grasses, herbs, and trees spread themselves both across the land and through the sea, the sky was turned into the luscious oxygen-filled air that we breathe today – or, at least, that we breathed up until the industrial revolution.

I enjoy reading the biblical creation story, contained within Genesis chapter one, in this way, and comparing it to how we believe life on Earth came to be. If read loosely, I think similarities begin to emerge. 'Heaven and Earth' could be space and time, separated out at the very beginning of our Universe into a place where we can move and one where we can't. 'Darkness and light' could signal the end of the opaque era, after which light was able to freely move. The land, sea, plants, fishes, fowl, and mammals all appear in Genesis in the order in which life on Earth began: our planet's cooling down from its hot formation, comets bringing ice and water, plants making the air breathable, and finally animals emerging from the deep. The similarities between this piece of ancient text and our modern understanding are uncanny, and I think that what we now know today about our planet's genesis and the origin of species lends a new lease of life to the scripture.

'Religion is a culture of faith; science is a culture of doubt.' So said Richard Feynman, the twentieth-century Nobel Prize winning physicist. If I am right, that there is so much in common between science and religion then why has a rift opened up between the two? If ancient religious texts can be read alongside modern science textbooks in this way, then why are an increasing number of people in Britain, particularly in the 18–24s age group, turning away from religion and towards science? Or is this question fundamentally wrong? Does asking why a person chooses science over religion or vice versa instigate a separation of the two, a false dichotomy? Are we setting up a conflict between science and religion that doesn't really exist?

Richard Holloway's dictum that the 'opposite of faith is not doubt, but certainty' contains the core of my own response to the science-faith divide. There are two points that I wish to make in response to this: that certainty in science is a barrier to faith, and that certainty in faith is a barrier to evangelism. The Holloway and Feynman quotes juxtapose nicely to illustrate these points. I think Feynman is really saying that religion is a culture of 'blind faith', of an acceptance of facts without questioning, and that this is contrary to any rational and scientific mindset. Holloway, on the other hand, seems to say that this could not be further from the truth. Certainty isn't the foundation of religion in his mind but its antithesis. Doubt and questioning are both crucial aspects of faith. I think Feynman and Holloway are both right as to the importance of doubt, for both science and religion, in our modern world, and the fact that they both accuse each other of certainty suggests that it is to blame for the perceived void between the two.

As technology becomes more firmly rooted in society, each of us lives in an increasingly small and more personalised online bubble, a world tailored to our personal beliefs. For many, news and information about the world come from the internet, and, in turn, the internet presents each of us with a careful selection of stories and links designed to entice clicks and capture our attention. 2020 has been an exceptional year for many reasons, one of which, that has mostly been absent from newspaper headlines, is the online spread of misinformation. COVID-19 conspiracies, vaccine fears, and, more recently, the spread of untruths in the run-up to, and aftermath of, the US Presidential Election have all featured prominently this year. I think the fact that so many of us are content to live in such narrow online worlds emphasises how fixed we are in our beliefs, how content we are to remain indifferent to other people's views of the world.

We seem to enjoy engaging with content that affirms what we already believe. I think this has probably been true for the vast majority of people throughout history. Humans are essentially conservative. Technology created even easier tailored worlds for each of us, with the internet answering our questions by holding up a mirror.

In Winchester, a city where I spent a large part of my childhood, there is a ledge in the cathedral around the inside walls on which people used to sit during services. In medieval times, the cathedral would have been overflowing with people during services, the floor packed right up to the walls. Why did so many come? Some will have simply wanted to get out of the cold, their minds shut to the words of the sermons. Many would not have understood the Latin words of the Mass. But some will have been open to new ideas and changing their minds.

Christianity grew out of Judaism and the teachings of a travelling Rabbi, Jesus of Nazareth. After his death, inspired by their sense of his resurrection and ongoing presence with them, his followers quickly formed into groups trying to live by his teachings. In the Early Church, as Christianity spread around the Mediterranean, there was lively debate about whether you had to be Jewish to be Christian. While a lot of Jews became followers of Christ, many more converts were gentiles, who found the story of Christ's life, death, and resurrection compelling. People can change.

What I think Holloway is getting at, when he speaks of certainty, is adhering, uncritically, to a particular interpretation of religion, and an unwillingness to recognise that much of religion is concerned with values, and value judgement. A large part of religion focuses on things that are unseen, and which can never be tested through scientific examination. This is a kind of ideological commitment rather than a lazy unwillingness to move on: if we have all the answers, then there is no need to keep seeking.

In another important sense, science demythologises religion. As technology expands and reaches more of the world, people become more aware of advances in science, medicine, and our understanding of the world, demystifying many questions as it does so. There is no need for Thor when we understand that static electricity causes thunder and lightning, and no need for Apollo when the sun is fuelled by hydrogen. The replacement of belief with a scientific understanding, however, can only account for that aspect of religion which seeks to explain the world around us. Science is yet to explain the meaning of life and morality. Perhaps the internet's negative impact, then, isn't the provision of accessible information, but the illusion that that information is self-sufficient and brings with it certainty. Online encyclopaedias, constant news, and countless online answers mean that each of us can feel as though we are an expert on the world: the origins of soap, or the names of the constellations, are only a few clicks away. It is hard not to feel an expert when you carry around so much information in your pocket. Technology has pushed each of us to become much more certain of our own world view, and has created a space where it is easy to find people who agree exactly with what we think, whether it is true or false.

Paul Tillich, the twentieth-century German-American Christian philosopher, provides another insight into the nature of faith when he says 'Doubt isn't the opposite of faith; it is an element of faith.' Why, I wonder, is the kind of popular, scientific certainty that I have described alien to religion? I believe we have become arrogant, self-righteous even, and that the certainty we find in modern science, and in the modern world as a whole, has made it more difficult for religion to own up to doubt. I don't wish to say that religion is malign, and feeds off doubt, but rather that, in order to have faith in something we cannot see, we must allow space in ourselves to consider that there may be things we cannot explain.

The scientific method, as my grandmother preaches, is founded on questioning and a constant, critical analysis of the world. Perhaps Science's questioning approach, the method of critical discovery, has become a new religion for atheists, replacing the doubt and questioning that Paul Tillich says is essential for belief. But if science is about questioning rather than certainty, then how can a certainty in science be to blame?

While travelling one summer, I came across a group of evangelists in Marienplatz in Munich, who had come together from across Europe and America to preach the gospel and convert people to their branch of Christianity. There, a born-again French missionary prayed for me, that I would have a safe journey home, and that my family would find God. I was told that no church would save me, and that I had to 'let Jesus into my heart' if I wanted to enter heaven. There was something appealing about that deep-rooted faith, that strong conviction she had in Christianity and in a way of life, but there was something alienating about it too, some inner voice that rose up within me and questioned the truth of her words. Perhaps what alienated me, and what I believe alienates so many, is the focus of evangelical Christianity on heaven, on salvation, and on the life of the world to come. I don't think the focus of religion on something that's intangible and invisible, such as the afterlife, is a problem in itself. Rather, I think the problem lies with the demand that people should believe with utter conviction in things which are inherently uncertain as if they were scientifically proven. There was no scope for doubting in her belief, nor in the belief of anyone preaching in that square: no room for change. For her, and for many Christians it seems, faith provides the certainty that many of us have placed in the modern world and in ourselves.

I frequently find this certainty among Christians alienating, and so too, I suspect, do my contemporaries. When people wish to spread the 'good news of the Lord', I find that they come across as pushy, too certain of themselves, too confident in the message they wish to proclaim. When evangelical ministers stand up and preach the gospel, they really are preaching to the converted. The congregation in front of them already believes every word they say, and are simply there, perhaps, to have their opinions bolstered. The preachers on the stage in that Munich square spoke to a rapt audience of flags and banners while tourists wandered disinterestedly past, stopping only to take selfies on their smartphones, and I believe that it was their certainty, the self-assurance of the preachers, that created the barrier between the two crowds. If faith is enhanced by engagement with doubt, then religion certainty lacks something. I suspect certainty in faith has risen in tandem with, or as a reaction to, the perceived certainty of empirical science. But the first step of the scientific method is always the question. Either way, I see it as an argument gone wrong, where both sides have dug their heels in too deep, refusing to question either themselves or what it even is that they started arguing about in the first place.

There are many different religions in the world today, and, even within the Christian faith, there are many different faces and theological interpretations. Who is to say that any one group is right?

I think facing up to disagreements is what is needed. Perhaps, in an age of certainty, of determinism, of having the world's knowledge at our fingertips, we need more questioning on both sides. If this sense of questioning, which is key to both faith and scientific reasoning, is to reach congregations, then ministers and evangelicals need to engage with those who doubt, not through self-assured proclamation, but through humble self-questioning. For the disenfranchised to find faith through the

Church, the Church must recognise how significant doubt is in the pursuit of faith. And, for those who claim the authority of science as a kind of superficial certainty, there must be a realisation that science is based on doubt and questioning.

Charles Darwin, the nineteenth-century naturalist, said, 'I am inclined to look at everything as resulting from designed laws, with the details, whether good or bad, left to the working out of what we may call chance.'

Physics is fundamentally uncertain. As you look at smaller and smaller particles, there is no way to determine how they will behave. At the quantum level, whether a particle decays, splits in two, or even where it is at any one time, is fundamentally uncertain and unknowable. The information, if it does exist, is beyond our reach, and the best we can hope to achieve is to describe the world in terms of probabilities. The everyday world we see around us is hence the sum of all these microscopic chances. Knowing and understanding that, at the most fundamental level, everything is uncertain, is perhaps what we need and what is missing from our modern outlook. Perhaps a greater appreciation, from both sides, that the Universe is inherently uncertain, can help to reintroduce much-needed doubt to religion, and help to bridge the gap between researchers and the clergy, between science and religion.

There's a chance, at least.

Faith vs Organised Religion

By Hannah Taylor

I was brought up as a churchgoer, not as a Christian. I say this because my parents didn't believe in God and had no intention for me to be Christian, but they made this decision for me because they thought it would be to my advantage. If I attended church from a young age, by the time I started Religious Studies at school I would have a strong grasp of Bible stories and would therefore be ahead of my peers. My second reason is that I did not have faith at that young age. Like many a small child, I believed in God because adults told me to. In my opinion this is not faith, though; faith has to involve a conscious decision on the part of the believer. For example, there is little reasonable doubt that Jesus lived and died – although there is no archaeological evidence, the gospels, and references in the writings of Jewish Historian Josephus and Roman Politicians Pliny and Tacitus give first-century testimony to the fact – but we have no concrete evidence that he was the Son of God and was resurrected three days after he died – that is faith.

Faith can also be separated from organised religion. I was a religious child but, on reflection, not a faith-filled one. It is, though, very easy to confuse the two, I maintained involvement with church through my teenage years, a time when many simply stop going. I became a sacristan and eventually chapel prefect at secondary school, a job that did me no favours when it came to popularity, and as a result I thought of myself as a Christian but, realistically, I was merely involved in organised religion. I thought I believed in God because I always had. My beliefs were not challenged by the outside world and I had no desire to challenge them myself, otherwise I risked having to give up something that was a huge part of my personality and my life. This fear was exacerbated by the fact I'm on the autistic spectrum. The Church (like many organised religions) is full of traditions and rituals, and as someone who finds comfort in repetition, routine and familiarity it's not surprising I was unwilling to give it up.

It was not until I started university that I was forced to re-evaluate whether I had a faith. Before arriving in Oxford, I didn't give much thought to the fact I was leaving behind the security of what I'd known before and disrupting eighteen years of routine and familiarity. I expected I would turn up, join the Christian Union (CU) and find a new church with little difficulty, when in fact the reality was very different. I found the main student churches didn't work for me and others looked too 'high church' for my liking, or seemed impossibly far away for an Oxford student to travel. In hindsight, my problem was I was looking for an exact replica of my church at home. To add to this, I was struggling in CU; the meetings involved praying out loud for one another and emphasis was placed upon inviting potential Christians to events. For me, the autistic who was teased at school for being religious, the level of social confidence this required was above me. Going home for Christmas eased my discomfort as I returned to my home church and the festive season swept me up. But by the time I returned to Oxford in January I was doubting the fundamentals of what I believed. This period was a crucial turning point for me: for the first time in my life, I truly considered whether I actually believed in God. I spent most of the term grappling with whether I was Christian because I believed or because it was what I'd always known. It was terrifying to imagine what I was without religion but, in the end, it was worth it because I came out with something more important, I finally had a faith.

In the meantime, I'd almost completely abandoned my search for a new church and my CU attendance became sporadic. I did spend some of the summer term attending a church that was as similar to my home church as I could find and I attended more

CU events, though not as many as I had at the start of the year. It was in the summer that I truly let my newfound faith grow. I was back at my home church and at the beginning of August I volunteered on a Christian Summer Camp for secondary school-aged children. I enjoyed it immensely: I was having Bible Study sessions three times a day in addition to a daily plenary service for the whole camp and I came out feeling truly closer to God and with a renewed enthusiasm for organised religion. The team I was part of were all young adults around my age and due to the nature of our roles – mainly involving washing up and preparing the dining rooms for all meals including breakfast – we all spent a lot of time together in close proximity. It is inevitable in these types of situations that friendships form quickly, and for me I left the camp with a new boyfriend. It was actually the first time I'd dated another Christian and this, along with my enthusiasm to get back in touch with organised religion, meant I started my second year of university with fresh enthusiasm, as though it was a second chance. I regularly attended the church I'd found at the end of first year and I made an effort to go to every CU event. But underneath it all was the underlying feeling that everything was not totally right.

It's strange to look back at that part of my life: I was trying so hard to tick all the boxes, be the perfect Christian, do what I thought was expected of me whilst burying the feeling that what I was doing *wasn't me*. The crunch point came about two-thirds of the way through term. I was attending something called 'Central', this is a fortnightly event run by OICCU (Oxford Inter-collegiate Christian Union) where all the college CUs come together. That particular week we were visited by members of OCCA (Oxford Centre for Christian Apologetics) and each OCCA member was running short Q&A sessions on different topics such as 'Suffering' and 'Forgiveness' that we could rotate around. I attended one on 'Sexuality', this was something I was particularly keen to listen to. In my last year of school, I had realised I was bisexual and have personally never found this to conflict with my faith. Obviously, I'm aware many Christians regard acting upon one's same-sex attraction as going against the teachings of the Bible.

I went to the discussion thinking that it would be an exploration of how sexuality and Christianity don't always have to conflict and, whilst that was the opinion of some, I was shocked to discover how many of the people of my age at that meeting started their sentences with 'well obviously homosexuality is a sin'. Perhaps I was naïve to think that homophobia in the church was limited to an older generation, but I was taken aback at the open 'us' and 'them' attitude taken by my peers. For me, this incident helped crystallise all that was wrong about the CU. I held different views and worshipped in different ways.

So, I left the CU, not loudly but quietly. I stopped turning up, clicked 'can't go' on *Facebook* events and slipped away into the shadows. This experience left me disconnected once more with organised religion in general and shortly after I stopped attending church in Oxford, not a decision I made consciously, other pressures of life took over until I no longer planned to go. Despite all this I felt strong in my faith. In the vacations I continued to attend my home church, and in Oxford I made contact with many of my fellow students who were also Christians and had distanced themselves from the CU, church or both.

This proved to be vital as I was about to experience the toughest period of my life. In the summer term of my second year one of my best friends experienced a relapse in his mental health, I'd known he'd had serious mental health crises in the past before I knew him. I spent a month as his main support/ carer. Others helped but I put my life on hold to help him, including a week where I slept in his spare bed when he didn't feel safe alone, only returning to my own room for flying visits to collect changes of clothes. If I wasn't in a lecture or labs or a tutorial, I was with him; when I wasn't with him, I worried constantly about his safety even if I knew someone else was looking after him. After a couple of weeks, the other people supporting him stepped back for the sake of their own health, so I spent even more time looking after him until that was all I was doing. On 3 June, 2017, two things happened, I turned twenty and my worst fears were realised when my friend made an attempt on his life. Unfortunately, his father and I found him too late, and despite our best efforts were unable to resuscitate him. My life crumbled around me as the reality of both the loss I had experienced and its traumatic nature started to sink in.

I could have easily abandoned God in the weeks and months that followed his death. I certainly questioned him, asked him why this had happened, but I held onto my faith. The routine of going to my home church that summer provided much needed comfort and my Christian beliefs in heaven and life after death helped me to deal with some of what I was feeling. When I returned to the same Christian summer camp as the previous summer, I was a shadow of myself but fully aware that my faith in God was what got me through the day. Unfortunately, I was not the only one to have changed, that year I discovered that the leader of our young adult team, and some of the other team members, held views similar to those I had seen in the CU and I was shocked at how openly they declared their homophobic views. I spent some very uncomfortable days in the knowledge that some of those with whom I was working so closely, fundamentally disagreed with a key part of who I was. The final straw came when the leader gave us a seminar on the different roles of men and women in the church and he made it very clear that he did not believe a woman's role was to lead worship, except maybe to children and other women, but definitely not as a member of the clergy. At this point I was ready to write off organised religion (except for my home church) for good. I was disheartened that the more I tried to engage with

Christian groups the more likely I was to uncover homophobia, misogyny and views which directly conflicted with my own. So, I did what any young person does in this sort of situation, I posted on a *Facebook* group. I'll admit I didn't know what I wanted to achieve apart from venting my feelings, but it did work. Someone commented and suggested a church in Oxford, minutes from my college that I had managed to overlook, so I decided to give organised religion one last chance.

That church was St Columba's a United Reform Church (URC). However, they not only had the normal Sunday morning service but also hosted a group called First Sunday. This group is a meeting of LGBTQ+ and questioning Christians of all denominations. Some further googling revealed to me that the URC is the only church in England to allow same-sex marriages in all its churches. Feeling hopeful that I had finally found somewhere with similar beliefs and values to my own, I gave it a go, and it was the right fit for me. This was a huge relief. It may have taken over two years but I'd finally found a church in Oxford that I clicked with. I spent my third year attending it, but in my final year attendance became sporadic because my boyfriend moved to a different university for his master's and weekends were spent visiting each other. But the difference between me when I started university and me now is that I no longer need organised religion. I spent so much of my time searching for the perfect church, feeling that if I didn't find it then would the disconnect from organised religion eventually lead to a disconnect from my faith. But now I've come through that period of my life I've realised it did the opposite; I now feel confident that whilst the right form of organised religion can supplement my faith, it isn't a necessary component.

Interestingly many young people belong to a faith yet don't engage with organised religion. It is something I have found remarkably more common than I initially realised. So why are so many of my peers leaving organised religion behind? This is a complex question with an undoubtedly complex answer, but I have come up with some possible contributing factors.

The first of which is a rather cynical point based upon my own experiences, but one can't help thinking that the religious environment of student life plays a part. As discussed earlier, I have had a negative experience with the Christian Union and I am not alone in this. The CU has many flaws, in my opinion, but the most relevant here is that it is an evangelical partisan Christian society yet does nothing to dispel the image that it is simply a student society for all Christians. With CUs up and down the country monopolising the student Christian society market, it makes sense to me that many young people walk away from organised religion when they don't fit into that mould. I am aware this is a very Christian specific issue and I feel so strongly about the damage that CUs can cause that I wrote an article for a student newspaper about it. It can still be found at www.oxfordstudent.com and search: 'OICCU: why leaving it behind was one of the best things I ever did for my faith'.

I think possibly that the principal reason for a lack of engagement in organised religion is the hectic nature of modern life. Life nowadays seems to demand a level of efficiency and productivity that can only be achieved if you are constantly on the go. Societal expectations of what constitutes being a modern, functioning adult are impossibly high and the effects of this can be seen in the increase in burnout in young people. When it all gets too much something has to give, and quite often organised religious can be the first to go. And why not? There's no quota or deadline you fail to meet by not going, there's no one to text saying, 'I'm really sorry I'm going to have to cancel.' You just don't go. I've personally found it especially difficult at university when sometimes I'd be deciding between finishing my work for the week or going to church; the work always won. Of course, it is not just young people who have busy lives but those of us under the age of 25 are just starting out in adulthood and are only beginning to form routines. Compared to someone in their fifties, perhaps a young person's routine is less ingrained and therefore more easily abandoned under pressure.

Another key factor is the shift that's occurred in cultural perceptions of organised religion. It used to be natural to assume that almost all members of society in Britain were involved in a form of organised religion. However, in the modern world it seems as though people are surprised to find you adhere to a faith at all, let alone engage in organised religion. It is no longer the cultural norm to engage with religion, whereas it used to be the case that those who didn't were met with shock or even distrust. Amongst younger age groups, religion is often perceived as something for the older generations; it's considered stuffy and old fashioned. There is also, I suspect, a link in people's heads between being religious and being socially conservative; the same assumption leads to associating the young with social liberalism. Of course, this prejudice does not necessarily hold true: many religious people are socially liberal regardless of age and many young people are socially conservative. However, the connection is made and it leads to surprise if a young person admits to being religious. It can even be a black mark against you in the eyes of your peers. I think many young people, consciously or subconsciously, shy away from organised religion in order not to be labelled as religious, in an attempt to avoid the negative connotations that can come with such a label.

Moreover, it is not just the way young people and society have evolved, but also how organised religions themselves have changed over the last couple of decades, that has affected how young people engage with them. As religion itself has become more of a niche in society, instead of a part of the everyday life of the nation, it has become more secluded. I think religion is now associated with those who are certain in their faith and highly religious in their practice. In the past those who were much less certain of their faith and unsure whether they fitted in, would not have been out of place in a religious organisation. The more casual attendee made up a large part of society. However, now these people may not feel comfortable in an environment where they are expected to show a driving desire to be an integral part of that religious community. At my home church attendance increases significantly at Christmas and Easter, and I think this is the result of people with a more casual relationship with religion being restricted to now only feeling comfortable attending services on important religious festivals. I think it's important to acknowledge the differences between faith and organised religion because there are so many, especially among my peers, who have distanced themselves from religion yet keep a spiritual curiosity.

So, what is the future of religion, will young people flock back to it or will they leave it behind for good? I think this very much depends on how religions themselves choose to move forward into our modern world. Organised religion has fallen out of favour with society and young people and whilst that is not the full fault of religions themselves, I do believe it is religions that will have to adapt to survive. The nature of this adaptation, though, is yet to be seen; what is it exactly that will entice the younger generations into being part of a religious community once more? I believe it could go one of two ways: more socially and theologically liberal or more socially and theologically conservative. The more liberal route seems to make more sense and is, personally, one I hope organised religions will take.

I mentioned the link society often makes between being young and socially liberal and, whilst this assumption does not universally hold true, I think many would agree it is generally the case. Perhaps it is because we younger adults have been born into a culture that has changed rapidly in the past twenty years, so, for example, the idea of gender equality is second nature to us. Or again, you might not encounter homophobic attitudes when you go to church, but gay marriage is still not permitted by most church denominations. Organised religions send out a message of social conservatism in their official stances. I believe this is the crux of the problem, religions are currently straddling a line where they want to seem as though they are becoming more progressive to keep the liberal members happy but don't want to become too progressive in fear of losing the conservative members. The result is that no one is truly happy.

On Being Brought Up Muslim

By Rumana Ali

Upbringing, mid-1990s to 2014

I was born in East London in the mid-1990s to Bangladeshi immigrant parents. Growing up, my parents constantly reminded me and my siblings of our cultural and religious heritage as South Asian Muslims, which I suspect was in part their way of asserting their own identity in a strange, unfamiliar country. While my parents set strict rules: no revealing clothes, no late nights out, and certainly no boys, they rarely enforced them with a heavy hand and often gave me the space to make my own choices. My house was adorned with Islamic symbols, like the images of iconic mosques on one of the free calendars that my dad brought back from the local mosque, while the adhaan or call to prayer was often heard from one of the five Bengali television channels that my parents regularly tuned into.

I went to an all-girls' comprehensive state secondary school that was a fifteen minutes' walk from my house. It was then headed by a Pakistani Muslim principal and had a significant Muslim and South Asian student population. I attended Muslim assembly in the mornings and, for my GCSEs, I studied Bengali instead of French – something my mum was very proud of. Most of my non-Muslim friends were Hindu, who shared a similar socio-economic and cultural background to me. After school, I went to a local mosque with my siblings and close neighbours to learn how to read Arabic and memorise verses of the Quran, the Islamic holy book. I regularly engaged in religious conversations with my friends and family about the meaning of life, the Day of Judgement, the afterlife, the life of the Messengers of God, and most fascinating of all, the supernatural world of the Jinn.

Growing up in Newham, an inner-city borough in East

London with a dynamic Muslim community, meant that I didn't feel I belonged to a religious minority during my childhood and most of my teenage years. As a child and teenager, I often felt disillusioned with the level of social deprivation in my borough, the high crime rate, and parochial feel. Today, although I continue to feel some of that disillusionment, I recognise that my identity as a British Asian Muslim is anchored in Newham, home to countless halal butchers, and an endless number of South Asian clothing stores that makes picking an Eid outfit a baffling ordeal.

It's difficult to say for certain whether I'd be Muslim without my upbringing. The thought that my belief in Islam, and by extension my chances of entering Jannah or Heaven, have been determined at birth is unsettling, as it seems arbitrary and undermines the concept of freewill, which is central in Islam. However, while it is possible, I was simply *born into* Islam, I choose it now and that's all that matters.

Leaving home for university, 2014–2017

Looking back now, I realise the world I inhabited as a child and teenager was small and insular. That changed in 2014 when at the age of eighteen I moved away from home for the first time to enrol as a History undergraduate at the University of Oxford. I was a first-generation student from an immigrant, working-class family; a state school student from a deprived borough; and, an ethnic and religious minority who had never before had a white or atheist friend.

From an early stage, I accepted that Oxford was going to be a challenge, and in more ways than one. Freshers' week, with its focus on drinking and clubbing, was particularly alienating. While students in my hallway stayed out late partying, I was either in bed by 10:00pm, at a less exciting 'alternative games' night at college, or at a social event hosted by the university's Islamic society. In both social and academic contexts, I felt culturally disconnected from most of my peers, who seemed more privileged than me. I became increasingly self-conscious about quirks I didn't realise I had, such as my East London accent, the slang I used, and my propensity to drop Islamic phrases like 'Masha'Allah' and 'Insha'Allah' into conversations.

At Oxford, I felt my Muslim identity come under scrutiny. My peers questioned me on choices that had been deep-rooted within my morality and way of life, and which I had rarely questioned, such as dressing modestly and not drinking alcohol. At times I felt challenged, even interrogated, by fellow students who sought to undermine the logic of my religious beliefs. But I was mostly met with genuine curiosity and an openness to learn. By justifying my choices and defending my faith, I began to lose the religious complacency I had grown quite accustomed to. I now found myself seeking halal food where it wasn't readily available, refusing alcohol that was offered to me at formal dinners, and being the only one who needed a moment to pray salah (one of the five daily prayers in Islam). I remember feeling that these actions were no longer just acts of worship, but of defiance against the *status quo*. Practising my faith at Oxford became the same as expressing my identity, and was a source of continuity with my upbringing and life back in East London.

There were various ways that I dealt with, though admittedly never overcame, the culture shock and alienation that I experienced at university. I focused on my studies and at times allowed myself to get lost in them, took frequent trips home to London during term, and hung out with fellow Muslim students. The Muslim societies at Oxford and Princeton University in the United States, where I spent a semester abroad during my second year, helped me navigate my Muslim identity in spaces that I struggled to claim as my own. As well as providing me with communal settings to practise my religion, they helped me let my guard down. I didn't have to justify my choices, feel like I was defending my religion, or worry about being judged.

Religion and spirituality: two sides of the same coin

As a child and pre-teen, I had a very black-and-white understanding of religiosity, believing that being religious was synonymous with being a good, moral person. However, whether it was through my exposure to religious hypocrisy or becoming friends with incredibly kind people who claimed to have no religion, I began to understand that conflating outward piety and moral goodness is deeply problematic. Practising religion isn't an end in itself but a means to becoming a good person, and is perhaps not the only route to getting there.

Religion and spirituality – that is, believing in an existence beyond the material world and having faith in a higher being – are two sides of the same coin. While I believe that it's possible to be spiritual without being religious, I also believe that practising religion allows individuals to reach their full spiritual potential. Due to the intangible nature of spirituality or faith, it's easy to be unaware of it. Religion allows us to align and reconcile our faith with our material existence. Muslim academic Reza Aslan stated that, 'religion is the language we use to express faith. It is a language made up of symbols and metaphors that allows people to express to each other (and to themselves) what is, almost by definition, inexpressible.' I largely agree with Aslan's hypothesis that religion is an outlet of faith, but I also find it quite oversimplifying and reductive. It suggests that faith is the prerequisite for religion and not vice versa, and therefore seems to deny the agency of religion itself. Religion doesn't just allow individuals to reinforce their existing faith but can guide them to discover it in the first place.

On the surface, the Islamic tradition seems to place greater emphasis on imaan or faith than on religious practice, as suggested by the hadith that 'no one will enter Hell in whose heart is an atom's worth of faith.' However, Islam also views faith as corruptible; it demands protection and nourishment through worship, and must be proven to God on the Day of

Judgement with good deeds. I've grappled with this tension my entire life, and have wondered whether it's enough to have faith in Allah without being a practising Muslim. My conclusion is always the same: my faith and religion are interdependent.

No religion counterbalanced by religiosity among immigrant communities, but for how long?

Immigrant and diaspora communities in the UK – many of which subscribe to non-Christian religions like Islam and Hinduism – seem to be shielded from the wider secularisation of the UK. British newspapers highlight that the decline in Christianity and rise in atheism in the UK are counterbalanced by the rise in Islam and heightened religiosity among Muslim communities. A recent study shows that London has a higher proportion of people identifying as religious than the rest of the UK, driven by the concentration of immigrant communities in the capital. According to *The Guardian*, this 'confound[s] perceptions of the capital as liberal and secular'. But this is not at all surprising.

Religion connects many immigrants and their families to their countries of origin, where it is often engrained within mainstream culture. They may therefore view their religion as an integral part of their cultural heritage and self-identity. Becoming atheist, or claiming to have no religious affiliation in these communities might be conflated with rejecting one's cultural heritage, and even disrespecting the immigrant experience. In western countries, however, religious attachments in immigrant communities are widely perceived as hindrances to social integration, while secularism is promoted as a prerequisite for it. British Muslims in particular have been scrutinised by the UK government and media for reportedly failing to integrate within British society. But studies have shown that 'millennial Muslims' are more likely than previous generations to live in ethnically mixed areas, hold more socially liberal views, and support social integration. It is possible that as younger generations of Muslims, and indeed of other religious minorities, become enculturated within British secular life, they will gravitate increasingly towards no religion, much like their Anglican peers. As older generations of immigrants disappear, and as 'intergenerational cultural dissonance' – a concept that refers to the clash between parents and children over cultural values, which is common among immigrant families – recedes, this does appear likely. Though, we'd need to wait a couple of decades to truly know.

So, while immigrant communities like mine appear unaffected by the trend of no religion in the UK *for the time being*, this might be a different story in years to come.

Glossary

Jinn: In Islamic tradition, Jinn are spirits with freewill who reside on earth, but cannot be seen by humans.

Masha'Allah: An Arabic phrase translated as 'God has willed it', used often to express appreciation, joy, or praise for an event or person.

Insha'Allah: An Arabic phrase translated as 'God willing', used often to refer to events that one hopes will happen in the future.

Hadith: A narrative record of the sayings or customs of Prophet Muhammad, who Muslims regard as the final Messenger of God.

Jesus Is a Feminist; Why Isn't the Church?

By Kizzy Jugon

For the record, feminism, by definition, is: The belief that men and women should have equal rights and opportunities. It is the theory of political, economic, and social equality of the sexes.
Emma Watson

Feminism runs in my generation's blood. We know we can do anything; we can be anything. I was allowed to hate dresses, love science, and read voraciously. We are incredibly privileged to live in the time that we do. Society has made strides to reconstruct what gender means – men are being encouraged to be more in touch with their emotions, women are told they can be leaders, and genders outside of the binary are being accepted into our common vocabulary. Throughout my 25 years, I have found female role models in real life and fiction. I learned Girl Power from the Spice Girls; to embrace academia like Hermione Granger; and to lean on fellow women, like the Halliwell sisters did. My parents work in the largely female-dominated nursing profession; my mother is in a more senior position than my father, and I saw him do nothing but support her.

Yet still, amongst the growth and changes, I felt the strains which society placed upon me as a woman. I never sought friendships with boys before university, because of the social presumption that I must want to date them. I was expected to spend significant amounts of money on hair removal and make-up to prepare for my daily role of 'human girl' before I was old enough to earn money myself. There was a double standard which still exists today, with sanitary products still being considered as 'luxury items' under tax laws while cake is considered 'essential'.

When we look at the Church of England with this lens of 'equality', the institution is far behind the curve. Women were only allowed to be ordained as priests in 1992 and as bishops in late 2014, and there are laws to protect those who disagree with the ordination of women, so they can selectively exclude them in their hiring processes. Popular narratives pit Christianity against feminist ideals: pro-life debates are characterised as restricting women's reproductive rights; the conservative Christian view of complementarianism promotes gendered roles which discourages women from being leaders of men; and conservative views on sex rival the feminist narrative of sexual liberation. These have created barriers between the message of the Gospel and the modern-day feminist and make it difficult to see how one could identify as both a feminist and a Christian. Yet here I am, making the bold claim that one can and should be both, because I believe in the Gospel and that God has made all human beings in His image and equal to one another.

The human mind plans the way, but the Lord directs the steps.
Proverbs 16:9

I wasn't raised in a religious family, and never anticipated that I would come to have a faith. My mother went to church as a child and regarded her Sunday school lessons as teaching her how to be a better, more valuable person to her community. My father had been a child immigrant in a strange country and Islam was his culture. As for my view: science could be proven, the existence of God could not, why would I trouble myself with something that probably didn't exist?

Morality, however, was important to me. I had to be kind, generous, and useful to others. I understood servanthood as a need to be smaller: a common narrative amongst women. We must not lead lest we risk being labelled as 'bossy'; our school uniforms must not distract the boys from their learning or the male teachers from their jobs; and we must be chaste lest our reputations be ruined forever. In my early teens I began to rebel against these ideals and identify with feminist ones, actively disagreeing with the Church which appeared to promote regressive narratives.

Virginia Woolf said, 'as long as she thinks of a man, nobody objects to a woman thinking.' She shows men as the subject and women as the object of society. It isn't hard to see how, as a young feminist, the idea of a male God being the ultimate authority over my life was an example of perpetuating the patriarchy that has suppressed women for so long. It is the exact opposite of what I was told to aim for – liberation and freedom.

Maybe I would have felt differently had one of the handful of church services I attended as a child taught me about Deborah. She was a prophet and a judge, which meant she had complete authority over the people of Israel, even at a hugely violent moment of its history. Deborah demonstrates an unexpectedly modern feminist ideal, which is comparable to current examples of female role models. She asked a warrior, Barak, to go to battle against Sisera, commander of the opposing Canaanite army. Barak requested that Deborah accompany them, and she replied:

'Certainly, I shall go with you,' she said, 'but this venture will bring you no glory, because the Lord will leave Sisera to fall into the hands of a woman' (Judges 4:9).

Deborah led Israel to victory, and Sisera ended up having a tent peg driven into his head by another woman, Jael. These are the godly warrior women we are shown in the Bible, but rarely told about. These are the strong, God-chosen women who are counter-cultural leaders, but our society doesn't know them.

It was at the end of a pretty tame university Freshers' Week that I asked, over a cup of tea, what my new friends were doing on our last day before term began. What followed was the weirdest conversation I had ever found myself in:

'You're going to church? Me too!'

'Oh my gosh, I didn't know you were a Christian too!'

It turned out that every friend I had made that week would be headed to church on Sunday morning, followed by a lunch with the congregation. What about me, the paradigmatic people-person, who didn't want her new friends to bond without her? Heck, yes, I was going too.

My first church service was... odd. We were greeted at the door by smiley students who handed out service sheets. I could handle this. There were a lot of people, a band which included drums, and I ended up sitting next to my new friends feeling completely out of place. It was a long service, I murdered the hymns, and the sermon was like a forty-five-minute lecture. It was striking how different this experience was compared with my other limited exposures to church (cold, dusty rooms full of people who looked like they were inches from their death bed). Here everyone was alive, joyful, and sure about something I didn't yet grasp. They also analysed the Bible like I'd been taught to analyse Shakespeare, which gave me pause. In my arrogance I assumed no intelligent person could actually believe any of this. Yet here was an academic approach to Christianity I had never seen before, and all of these seemingly bright people genuinely believed that this was an authentic source. I had to go deeper.

Mary is the only woman of the Bible I knew much about from an early age but I did not identify with her. A young girl, probably 12–14 years old, was visited by an angel and told she was going to get pregnant by the Holy Spirit and that her son will be the Messiah who will save humankind. It is really difficult to imagine what this girl must have been thinking, but what we do know is that she gives her consent to her part in this plan:

Then Mary said, 'Here am I, the servant of the Lord; let it be with me according to your word' (Luke 1:38).

While this theme of consent fits the modern feminist narrative, the gendered role of motherhood is not as favourable to the feminist view. Mary is the most prominent woman in the Bible, and we are not told of any particular gifts she has, all we know is that she is faithful, a virgin, and able to bear children. Here, I think, lies the church's main mistake: presenting Mary as the female role model to Christian women, it presents her as the principal example for the concept of Christian womanhood.

There are so many problems with this, one being that if women are called to bear children where is God in miscarriages or infertility? This also contradicts Paul's teachings later in the New Testament glorifying singleness and presenting marriage (and therefore having children) as a second-best solution if one cannot control oneself enough to remain single (1 Corinthians 7:8–9).

My first two months of university led me further into the rabbit hole. I was attending Bible studies, church services, Christian Union groups, and attempting to do a medical degree. It was slowly driving me up the wall. Everyone was so certain that God was real and that he could solve all of my problems, and nobody shied away from my questions: they were grateful when I asked a question they could not answer – 'It is good to doubt or be unsure, it's how we grow,' they said. These people prayed for me, consoled me, ate with me, shared their lives with me, and seemed genuine in what they said and did. I just could not figure them out.

Ultimately, I realised I would have to make a leap of faith and decide whether I believed that God was real, whether there was something more. Oddly enough, this leap came during a discussion with my atheist medical student cohort. We were considering consciousness, and how science explains this as a series of neural processes influenced by genetics and our environment. They say our very being can be whittled down to electrons moving in certain patterns along biological circuit boards, but I knew that this wasn't the full picture. I believed that I was more than just a reaction of certain molecules to a set of stimuli; I was a person with emotions, a conscience, and an ever-surer belief in loving people in spite of the cost to oneself. I had to admit that there was more to the world than what science could tell me.

> *For there is no distinction, since all have sinned and fall short of the glory of God; they are now justified by his grace as a gift, through the redemption that is in Christ Jesus.*
> Romans 3:22–24

I remember the first time I felt God's presence. I was in a café, in the middle of a one-on-one Bible study on Romans 3:20–24. St Paul wrote to the Romans and summarised the Gospel in a few short sentences: essentially, nobody is perfect, but only the sinless get to heaven, because God cannot look upon those with sin. So, God sent his Son, Jesus Christ, to Earth to live a sinless life and die as a perfect sacrifice for all of us. By accepting this sacrifice, we are washed clean and can have a relationship with God. This gift is described as grace. If you want to get to heaven, accept that the payment has been made for you and give your consent, because you are loved more than you can possibly imagine.

The moment I grasped what grace actually was, I felt God. It was a familiar feeling of being loved by another person and being completely safe with them; it was like I was a child again with my head in my mother's lap as she stroked her fingers through my hair. I was terrified. I said nothing to the person I was with. I had found the exact opposite of what I had set out to find. God was real, and He loved me. I wanted to run in the complete opposite direction.

It was when I was at home in the Christmas vacation that everything shifted. Quite literally, because my family had moved out of our home and into the first of a series of temporary accommodations which left me living out of boxes for a while.

I did not have a church at home, or Christians to pray with, or another excuse to contact a God I now knew to be real. Without the church I had found at university, it was up to me to keep my relationship with God going. But I wasn't ready to say that out loud yet, and I couldn't go to church without talking to my family. So, I found myself praying to God one night, 'Right, I believe in you now, I know that you're there and that you did this amazing thing in sending Jesus to die for my sins, but now what? What is it I need to do to become a Christian, because honestly I'm lost.'

It turns out that, anticlimactically, I had done everything I needed right there.

I decided promptly I wouldn't tell anyone I believed in God until they asked. I was unprepared for the joy I would face upon telling my church family; their excitement was infectious. For my home friends, it felt entirely different because I didn't know how they would react. When a friend 'came out' to me as a lesbian, I 'came out' as a Christian, both of us expecting the other's rejection but being wonderfully disappointed. It was a night of mutual celebration and safety for us at the age of 19, in an empty car park, in the early hours of the morning.

> *You may not control all the events that happen to you, but you can*
> *decide not to be reduced by them.*
> Maya Angelou

My first year as a Christian was filled with difficulty. I struggled in my university exams, had panic attacks, and felt this deep sadness that I couldn't identify the cause of. My friends kept me going, Christian and non-Christian. They reminded me of the good in the world, and they gave me the support my broken family couldn't at that time. But I still hadn't learned the art of talking to others when I struggled, and it meant I got into a cycle of pushing so many thoughts and feelings down that I was running out of space to fit them all.

A friend of mine describes Oxford University as a constant fear of drowning. She says that if you are barely keeping your head above the water that means you're doing fine. I lived on a diet of coffee and medical school essays, but managed to get enough oxygen to survive. I scraped through first year and returned to my second year, living in a more isolated place and leaning on my friends with accommodation closer to my college. Home was a stressful place that even medical school couldn't compete with, so the term time with my friends kept me going.

I trusted my friends, I depended on them, until one of them sexually assaulted me. The first time it happened someone stopped him and told him he was going too far, and that was that. I didn't stop to think about it. It was fine at first, then it wasn't. I'd asked him to stop and he hadn't, I'd had to ask another friend to intervene. But then it was over. No big deal.

The second time was my breaking point. A different friend was there and responded to my outrage. I got away and I hid in another room until someone I trusted came home. Our 'misunderstanding' was smoothed over, I began to feel safe again, surrounded by other friends, but I never wanted to see the man who had assaulted me again. It turned out that the feeling was mutual, with barbs thrown my way whenever we were together in a social situation – we had mutual friends and went to the same college, so it was difficult to avoid. I distanced myself from the people I loved most in college, who didn't take it well when I retreated to my church and medical school friends.

I spoke to members of my college welfare team about what had happened to me. But the perpetrator was a Christian, well known by those I had spoken to, and I felt like they saw me as someone trying to cause trouble. 'Be careful with what you're saying,' I was told. 'He is a respected member of the

Christian community here; you could ruin him.' Believing I was overreacting, I felt guilty for saying anything. Nobody else in my friendship group had an issue with this man, and they all knew what he had done to me. I thought I had no other option but to try and move on.

I don't blame them for not understanding, this was before the #MeToo movement and none of us had the vocabulary to describe what had happened as 'sexual assault'. If it wasn't rape, it was fine. I was a Christian, everyone was broken, and the right thing to do would be to forgive, right?

When I turned to the Bible, I found Tamar's story:

Amnon took hold of Tamar, and said to her, 'Come, lie with me, my sister.' She answered him, 'No, my brother, do not force me; for such a thing is not done in Israel; do not do anything so vile! As for me, where could I carry my shame? And as for you, you would be as one of the scoundrels in Israel. Now therefore, I beg you, speak to the king; for he will not withhold me from you.' But he would not listen to her; and being stronger than she, he forced her and lay with her.
2 Samuel 13:11–14

Tamar was raped by her half-brother, Amnon, and her father David did not punish him because he loved his firstborn son. Afterwards, Amnon was so filled with hatred that he had Tamar thrown out of the room by a manservant. In the end, Tamar's other brother, Absalom, orchestrated Amnon's death to avenge her treatment. It is one of many stories of assault in the Bible.

Tamar's sense of shame resonates with every survivor of sexual assault and I have clung to this passage when I revisit my experiences. Where do we carry the shame? There is a narrative in some churches, especially those that preach no sex before marriage, that purity and virginity are of absolute importance. Sexual sin is seen as far worse than any other 'for the fornicator sins against the body itself' (1 Corinthians 6:18).

This kind of teaching can be so harmful to women, whether survivors of sexual violence or not. The world has moved beyond parents hanging bloodied bed sheets outside of their window after their daughter's wedding night. Virginity is not a quality to aspire to – like humility, loyalty, or honesty – just a word attached to lacking an experience, consensual or otherwise. Virginity does not give us value. You do not lose something when you graze your knee for the first time; it is the getting back up and running again which gives us growth of character. The man who assaulted me did not take anything from me; he just opened my eyes to the risk of being a woman in the world. Men like him are the reason I have a contraceptive implant: I do not want to have an abuser's child or get an abortion. The fact that women must think of these risks proves how far away from biblical and feminist ideals we still are.

My church failed me in my abuse. A crime requires motive, means, and opportunity and I was taught that by giving opportunity to this man *I* was at fault. Today, it is estimated that 30% of partnered women have experienced physical and/or sexual violence from a partner at some point in their lives.[1] As Margaret Atwood put it, 'Men are afraid that women will laugh at them. Women are afraid that men will kill them.' We need women to be an integral part of the church at all of its levels, so that the people who understand the risks that women face can help fix them.

I did not realise how difficult my secular friends in college had found my churchgoing until the day before my baptism, when they staged an *intervention* in which they informed me I was being baptised into a sexist and homophobic church, that I had been brainwashed, and that I was pulling away from them. To be fair I *was* pulling away, just not from them, but from the man who had assaulted me, with whom they still spent time. Their arguments were familiar to me: the church I attended at the time was vocal in their opposition to the ordination of women and same-sex marriage. But I have always believed that women should be priests and that same-sex marriage (or, as I call it, *marriage*) should be celebrated in the church. My baptism was not about the views of any one church; it was about me going to the river (conveniently next to a rather nice pub) alongside people from several churches and making public vows that I believe and trust in one God: Father, Son, and Holy Spirit.

Every single one of my non-Christian home friends came or signed a card congratulating me; medical students sat by the river in a gaggle; and my mother and little sister even made the trip from my hometown. None of them understood why I was doing what I was doing, they just loved me more than they cared to disagree. We sat by the river, I was dunked in, and then we all went to the pub. It was one of the happiest days of my life.

I have come to regard with some suspicion those who claim that the Bible never troubles them. I can only assume this means they haven't actually read it.
Rachel Held Evans

It was the summer after my second year of university that I began the inevitable tumble. I had spent an amazing few weeks volunteering in Haiti with a Christian organisation. I enjoyed the weather, the people, and was delighted how happy the orphanage boys were when we finished their dormitory and they exchanged the floor of their wooden shack for rooms with proper beds. I began a lab project working on cancer research; this was the sort of summer that would impress others, the kind that only a top-level university could give you access to. But my mental health was failing, and as the summer came to a close more and more friends from college came back to Oxford, beginning another year of battling with the constant pressures from friends to abandon my church, to spend time with the man who assaulted me, and to do well in my degree.

God felt so far from me at this point. Home hadn't improved as much as I needed it to, work was difficult, and I had been assaulted by a Christian. I didn't feel God in this. Where was He when we suffered? What about those living with war, poverty, or illness like those I had spent time with that summer? Where was God then?

Suffering is a part of life everyone struggles with, and as a Christian it's easy to blame God when things beyond our control go wrong. Bathsheba and her experiences provided comfort for me. David was a king heralded as a hero of the Jewish faith, but he was as broken as any human is. He had an affair with Bathsheba, got her pregnant, and orchestrated her husband's death. God killed the child to punish David for his evil ways and David accepted the punishment. Bathsheba's heartache is shown through David's comfort of her, but is largely left to the reader's imagination.

So often, the suffering we blame on God has a far more human cause. In this case, though, the punishment is a result of David and Bathsheba's adultery, we know that David has significant power over Bathsheba, and these unequal dynamics mean that she has little choice in her situation. Consent relies on someone's ability to say 'no' and Bathsheba could not say no to a king. Men are in positions of power in the Old Testament, to the point where the Hebrew words translated as 'husband' include 'master' (as in, of slaves). Current Bible translations continue to favour the male lens, for example, 'So God created humankind in his image... male and female he created them' (Genesis 1:27).

This passage is often quoted as 'so God made man in his image' and leaves out the mention of women all together, assuming that the reader understands that 'man' means 'humankind'. This is problematic because if asked to name 'men' in the Bible not many would name 'Mary' or 'Ruth', and excluding an explicit mention of 'female' could exclude women from the narrative of God's plan entirely. This verse is the beginning of establishing God's love for all who He created to be like Him, so must explicitly include women in that.

These examples are just some of those which discouraged me as a feminist Christian. The Church seemed to be interpreting God's word as a means to view women, if they are viewed at all, as less than men. But that is not what we are presented when we look at scripture closely. When we are suffering, we are vulnerable and the Church has a responsibility to remind all of us of our indisputable value to God who loves us perfectly, regardless of our sex. My church did not do this. That summer, it took over an hour of rapid breathing to admit to myself that I was having a panic attack, and that I had been having them for years. I needed to take time off, I couldn't sit my exams, and I couldn't go back to a place where I was this unsafe again.

I felt like a failure. I couldn't find God in my life without doubting His intentions. I had been assaulted by a Christian, rejected by Christian friends, failed by my church, and everything else seemed to be going wrong. I couldn't see how I had got to this point if God really loved me as He was supposed to. I felt like I must have done something to deserve to feel like the world would be better without me in it.

What began as one year out of university became three. I'm not good at expressing my worries to others – not serious ones – and that made my recovery go much slower. I turned to self-harm when things got too difficult, I barely slept at night, and could easily sleep through all the daylight hours. The panic attacks were the worst, especially when I'd woken from a nightmare, convinced that the man who assaulted me was there.

It was at a particular low point, at the urging of a friend that I turned to the Bible and read the gospels. I discovered that Jesus was a radical figure of his time, in part because he was a feminist. He empowered women and cared for them regardless of their social status or background. It was Jesus who challenged the definition of adultery – 'I say to you that everyone who looks at a woman with lust has already committed adultery with her in his heart' (Matthew 5:28) – and refused to order the stoning of a woman caught committing adultery. Instead, he pointed out that everyone sins, and that regarding a woman's sexual sin as worse than their own is self-deception.

Jesus forgives a 'sinful woman' because she is repentant, and speaks to a Samaritan woman who has many husbands of the salvation that she, a foreigner, is now entitled to. Jesus broke the barriers between gender, race, and the sinful. He saw people for who they truly were, imperfect but loved infinitely by God. He resolved the inequality created in the curse of Genesis 3:16 – that the husband will rule over the wife as a punishment for disobeying God. He promises that the last will be made first and the first will be made last.

Churches should follow this teaching, but often manage to miss the mark. If they were to act as Jesus did, as true feminists, they could reach a generation aiming to accept difference and create positive change. It took me three years to disclose my assault to a professional, because of the shame I felt. People in this situation need understanding, love, and support, not to be silenced and told they have lost something in having sexual experiences (consensual or otherwise); and it is so important that churches don't ignore the women in the Bible who experienced these things.

I was well into my recovery when I had a revelation: I was 23 and I was bisexual. Therapy had helped me to change my thought patterns, so I was more comfortable looking at myself and it showed through the new friendships I made and the old ones I strengthened. I realised this as I claimed Oxford back as my own, and not just as a place where I was sexually assaulted. I turned to the Bible, my LGBTQI+ friends, and the one Christian friend who had been at my side throughout my recovery. They all offered me nothing but love and support. Whatever happened, I was loved and I was cared for. I was not alone in this.

I'm aware that I'm at an advantage compared to many – I've never doubted that my family would still support me in a same-sex relationship. For once, my worry was more for the reaction of my heavenly 'Father' than my biological one. The church where I had first found Christ had a hard line on their views of 'same-sex attraction'. The preacher is well known as someone who experiences 'same-sex attraction' and chooses to live celibately as a result. While, as a bisexual woman, I had more freedom because it was possible for me to fall in love with and marry a man, it didn't mean that it wasn't important to explore these homosexual aspects of myself from a Christian perspective, from **my** perspective.

In my research I found Ruth, a widow who features in the genealogy of Jesus. Despite being a foreigner, she was welcomed by Boaz, who treated her kindly, gave her a job and ensured she was treated well by others. Ruth was later encouraged by her mother-in-law, Naomi, to lie next to Boaz one night and uncover his 'feet' (read: genitals), leading him to seek her hand in marriage. I can't unravel the cultural oddities this story gives us here, but I can say that Ruth owning her sexuality in this way feels very modern: she knew who she wanted and pursued them. The Song of Solomon unfolds similarly, with a female narrator unapologetically seeking her lover.

My beloved is mine, and I am his.
Song of Solomon 2:16

The equality of the ownership expressed here is radically different to that shown in the lord-slave model for marriage that we saw in the Hebrew of the Old Testament. It is also a woman's perspective, a rarity in these texts, and shows women having positive sexual experiences in which the aim is not purely procreation, but an act of love created by God to be a part of the human experience. These women showed me that there was no shame in being bold regarding their sexuality and reminded me that sex was created by God and we should celebrate it.

Embracing the feminist message of the Bible was becoming increasingly central to my faith, and in the end, it was the cost of growing to love people who would stand against women being in positions of authority in the church, and gay Christians ever getting married which led me to seek a different church. The people I had worshipped with supported something that damned a part of me, a part I knew I couldn't change, one that, through study of scripture and prayer, I have determined is as much a part of myself as being female, mixed-race, and extroverted. God made me in His image, I am one of His children, and I am fearfully and wonderfully made. To believe that is the most liberating thing in the world. I am secure in my identity in Christ, and in the knowledge that God will steer me, through scripture, prayer, worship, and my trusted friends, to do the best that I can. While I know that I will make many, many mistakes, I don't believe that being accepting of my sexuality is one of them.

Despite the obstructions created by some of the teachings of the Church, the Bible itself proves that to be a Christian is to be a feminist. My generation needs to hear about all the different women praised in the Bible that we relate to and who walked with God. In teaching about these women, the Church will show the inclusivity of the Gospel rather than painting Christians as picketers outside of abortion clinics; protesters at LGBTQI+ Pride marches; and perpetuators of patriarchal ideals. It is vital that the Church takes responsibility for loving women and showing them the nature of God through its actions, because it reflects the core message of scripture:

Jesus said to him, 'You shall love the Lord your God with all your heart, and with all your soul, and with all your mind.' This is the greatest and first commandment. And a second is like it: 'You shall love your neighbour as yourself.'
Matthew 22:37–39

Notes

1. This study excluded emotional and psychological violence. Source: 'Global and regional estimates of violence against women: prevalence and health effects of intimate partner violence and non-partner sexual violence.' World Health Organisation

Keeping Up with Catholicism

By Nora Baker

When I was about seven or eight, I remember asking my mother, during a visit to a grand-aunt's house one day: 'When I'm old, will I become really religious, as well?'

I was used to visiting elderly relatives' houses filled with Catholic symbols – St Brigid's Crosses hanging over doorways, miniature holy water fountains to bless oneself on leaving the house, Child of Prague statues and framed cross-stitched hymns. Most of those over sixty went to Mass every single day and made a special event of the Novena. My house, in contrast, had just one picture of the Sacred Heart – with no glowing red light in front of it – and the holy water fountain tended to hang dry on the wall. We only went to Mass on Sundays and official Holy Days of Obligation. And, so, I'd learnt to associate more determined and hard-core religiosity with those of a certain age. I had presumed it was something I would grow into, a slow, transformational process reserved for grandparental figures, developing dedication like developing wrinkles or an unsteady gait.

My childish question that day did not inspire much introspection on the part of my parents: instead, I received a half-joking admonition for inferring that my relation was old. I sometimes find myself looking back, however, to that observation of generational differences in religious experience. I think back on the proliferation of religious symbols throughout Ireland that I used to witness as a child, especially nowadays as they begin to dwindle in number. When my family had an extension built onto our house, the Sacred Heart picture was not put up again, and the walls by the doorway now boast a coat rack instead of a place to bless oneself. My father's car no longer has a sticker of Padre Pio in the window above the tax information, and the Child of Prague statue seems to have been removed from the window of the home he grew up in following my grandmother's death. In the increasingly fast-paced, globalized world that has been my home since my teenage years, there seems to be less time or space to focus on formal prayer and rites. And, though I perhaps have a more religious-inclined background than most, my peers and I have not known anything like the strict Catholic conservatism of our grandparents' or even our parents' youth.

In the wake of scandals and surges in socially liberal views, antagonism against the Church has been increasing in Ireland since the late 1990s. Those in their twenties and teens are more likely to associate Irish Catholicism with a system that abuses power and restricts personal freedoms. Yet nearly every person of my age will have undergone major rituals such as receiving the sacraments of Baptism, Confession, Communion and Confirmation, and revelled in them as major milestones and family events. They are likely to have participated in classroom prayers and school Masses – I recall that, in secondary school, some of the most earnest candle-holders and psalm-readers during holy ceremonies were those who self-identified as atheist. For some members of my generation, there may be a personal spiritual dimension to this kind of ritual participation, even if it might not be considered 'cool' or 'woke' to admit it.

However, while I cannot read the minds and intentions of every young person I know, I can at least speak to the sentiments of popular mood that I've picked up from conversations with peers, and from trends in Facebook 'memes' and student newspapers. And the mood I detect indicates that much of the reason why Catholic tradition remains important to young Irish people of my age is its connection with their sense of national identity, rather than being a case of pure religious affiliation.

This is not to say my peers and I only experience spirituality in terms of latent nationalism. Many say that while they may not have much time for organized religion, they do believe in some kind of 'higher power'. They may not be certain of its form or nature, but most young people I know say they feel that 'there is something out there'. And, though most may not formally kneel or pray, the majority may take time to pause and reflect in other ways, perhaps by engaging in meditation, writing, or listening to or performing music. I think that religious practices have always changed over time, but aspects of humanity tied to religion – from introspection to self-righteousness, from works of love to those of hatred – would appear to have remained fairly constant. One of the main roles religious beliefs have played through the years has been to address our queries as to why we are here, what we are doing, and what we should do. However, I think young people today tend towards 'science' for the answers to these questions.

Social Context

Virtually every school in Ireland is run by a religious order – though there are fewer and fewer nuns and priests among their teaching staff these days, and secularization is spreading slowly but surely. However, if there were to be talk of restrictive sex education based on religious morals, I suspect there would be public uproar. Not much mention was made of non-heterosexuality when I was in school, but we were told, during a sexual health talk, that we should love and support those who came out to us.

I mention this because I think it illustrates how different the world I inhabit is to the one my parents grew up in. Homosexuality was only decriminalised in Ireland in 1993. Divorce was brought in by a referendum two years later: this overturned a previous referendum outcome of 1986 in which nearly 64% had voted to maintain its constitutional ban. I understand that artificial contraception wasn't widely known in Ireland until the 1980s. When Gay Byrne, a popular late-night talk show host, introduced his audience to a condom one evening on a 1987 edition of his programme, channels across the country were switched. Many tutting noises and complaints were made. As I grew older, I began to learn more about the history of the relationship in Ireland between Church and State, between social conservatism, and sex. Though it has rarely occurred to those of my generation to look upon extramarital relations as a mortal sin, many towns across Ireland still bear the buildings of former Magdalene Laundries, a stark reminder of the past and recent source of public outrage. These were institutions for those described as 'fallen women' and saw 10,000 young females pass through them between 1922 and 1996. Run by orders of nuns, the Laundries were a mixture of workhouse, asylum, and home for unmarried mothers. As penance for their crime of fornication, these women were made to work all day washing clothes, and were not allowed out into wider society.

The rigid rules of the past may seem equally alien to youth on either side of the Irish Sea, but in Ireland the memory of the banishment of unwed mothers feels more recent. Most of my friends' families here in England appear to have been raised without religion and therefore approach religion from the perspective of indifference or curiosity. I think it is more difficult for Irish young people to feel this level of detachment from organized religion. This is not just because they are less likely to have had a secular education, but because the memory of the betrayal felt when the abuse scandals started coming to light is still so fresh. This memory is still fresh because the betrayal was so deep, and the betrayal cut so deeply because the trust put in religious leaders was so absolute – they could do next-to-nothing wrong. I would therefore argue that most Irish people of my age approach organized religion with a mixture of familiarity – because of a childhood spent singing hymns and practising proper walks for Communion Day – and suspicion.

Many young people (as well as old) feel righteous anger about abuses of power on the part of the Catholic Church in the past. However, though leaders within the church may be associated with wrongdoing, for many, its rituals, songs, and pomp are endearing. They are deeply embedded in our culture, as we see with large family celebrations of First Holy Communions and Confirmations. The parties surrounding these sacraments can see children receiving hundreds of euro as presents from family friends and relatives, and the dress code recalls that of a wedding.

When it comes to these flamboyant traditions, Catholic Ireland perhaps has more in common with Spain or Poland than the rest of the British Isles. I believe that in Ireland, the perpetuation of these rituals is linked to what I would call 'small nation syndrome'. As a country, Ireland finds itself geographically positioned between larger, Anglophone, wealthy G7 countries. Desperate to assert its identity on the world stage, it objects to being confused with its next-door neighbour, Northern Ireland, in particular, and Irish citizens find themselves trying to project what it is about their culture that makes it unique, what makes them different from America or Britain. Nationalism is a strange and messy concept. Trying to untangle it, I think most Irish people would identify more with a civic nationalism rather than the ethnic nationalism promoted by right-wing groups.

In years gone by, priests may have been considered figures of high authority, but that is not normally the case now. Most parishioners find themselves on roughly equal footing when it comes to piety – self-righteous souls notwithstanding. If an Irish language upbringing is not a common denominator for the youth of today, an Irish Catholic upbringing is. Religious diversity is still so seldom seen in rural Ireland that just about all children of the same age in a small village find themselves making their First Holy Communion together, attending Mass in their Communion dresses and suits on the feast of Corpus Christi a month later, and, four years after that, making their

Confirmation together. Factors such as satellite television, the internet, cheap airflights and mobility grants for study abroad have increased awareness that things are different elsewhere. Exposure to more secular customs and upbringings in other countries have highlighted the absurdity of some Irish Catholic rituals, but it also somehow gives them a special place in the hearts of the millennial generation. Some traditions may seem antiquated, but they, unlike the Irish language, are a level playing field for just about all Irish citizens, a marker of identity easier to relate to oneself or to one's family.

Even the darker side of Church belief can be sentimentalised by young Irish people in the search for national identity. For example, there is the belief that babies who died before baptism go to a purgatory known as 'limbo', and thus could not be buried in official cemeteries. Then there are the shock horror stories, such as the discovery of new-born bodies inside a septic tank at a disused mother-and-baby home in Tuam. We often showcase these occurrences to non-compatriots in part to shock them, but also to assert and acknowledge, in a strange sort of way, that this is part of our shared 'Irish' national history. Some parts of this history may be ugly, but it is unique, not immediately discernible to 'outsiders' – even if they hail from countries that are close neighbours. Mocking of elements of the Catholic past stand-up routines can often have a targeted purpose behind it. Humour is frequently used as a tool to define in-group and out-group boundaries. When young Irish people discursively link themselves to Irish tragedies, such as the Tuam Babies scandal, they are implicitly positioning themselves in a group distinct from others in the world.

Religion may not be chief among the topics parodied in popular Irish Facebook groups such as 'Ireland Simpsons Fans', 'Brexit' barbs and Barry's tea debates tend currently to reign supreme. But Irish Catholicism certainly is a common source of satire. Posts on Child of Prague statues and the 'ALIVE-O' series of children's Catholic school books promote a sense of group childhood nostalgia. Magdalene Laundries become the target of biting righteous satire. Shared memories and outrage related to religion bond Irish citizens from opposite ends of the state in the way it seems shared fondness for the food chain Gregg's bonds citizens of England's North.

The relationship between genuine spirituality and official pomp and circumstance is difficult to discern among Ireland's youth. But faith is such a personal thing that perhaps it is right that there be such a disconnect. Some believe we should not deviate from doctrine; others find more solace in birdsong than in scripture. I do hear many people my age say that it's more important to *be a good person* than to be religious. I tend to nod my head in response, because I agree that faith and kindness are not intrinsically linked, although the highly subjective nature of the word good makes their statement a little opaque.

Perhaps it is hypocritical to label oneself as a religious adherent if one does not follow all its tenets to the letter. Recently I debated the nature of true religion with an undergraduate friend. They argued that those who engage in homosexual relations, or blaspheme, cannot be 'real' Christians or 'real' believers of any tradition that teaches these things are wrong. I would argue, however, that it is impossible for humans to live truly 'by the book'. Even if one believes in written words with all one's heart, there is a fundamental irreconcilable distance between language and action. We can describe what we do and dictate what we should do, but we are attaching letters and sounds to bodily functions – the relationship was not naturally there, it was human-made. We can try to be as pious as possible, but it isn't possible to live a real life according to words, when words are shaped by our actions, rather than the other way around. What is language other than a system of signs and symbols designed to express the human experience? It is obviously possible to use words to dictate action, but I think our emotions are too complex to be infallibly governed by the prescriptions of doctrine. And I think God accepts this; he doesn't expect us to be perfect but encourages us to reflect on what we've done and how we can be better.

Personal Experience

I am not sure where to define myself on the scale of religious belief. At times I find it difficult to discern which aspects of my life relate to Catholic beliefs and which are just natural human processes. Where is the line between ritual and routine? However, I think the social aspect of religious practice has played a large part in my life, as has the presence of the religious idolatry I have described. In my local parish in Ireland, I associate attending Mass with family and family friends. Most of these individuals are much older than me, but that does not mean I do not feel I benefit from my relationships with them, and hopefully the opposite is also true.

In Oxford, it is somewhat different. I am in a city instead of a rural village, with several churches and various Mass times to choose from, and it is unlikely I will meet people I know, no matter which I attend. I think this contributes to the feeling of fraud, in a way – something in me fears that those I shake hands with may think that, because I am a young person, I am not serious about faith in the way that they are. Perhaps I am not, and perhaps I fear they may detect this somehow and judge me for it, though I know logically that does not make sense.

One evening last year, I found myself participating in a Sunday Mass following a sexual encounter. I looked around at those in other pews and aisles, thinking of how they were unaware of what I had done the night before, wondering how they would react if they discovered my premarital relations and wondering what sins of their own they hid and whether they bore any similarity to mine. I stayed behind to make additional personal prayers following the ceremony and pondered how I could make amends for what I had done so as to be considered 'good', even by those with more traditionalist views. Would it be better to take more time to participate in rituals of fasting and confession, could prayer cancel out indulgences? Or should I instead try to spend time being as selfless as possible by volunteering and taking action instead of daydreaming and fussing? It was not until sometime after that I realised I was not thinking of how my actions would be seen in God's eyes, but how they would be considered by those around me. We may be told to love our neighbours, but I was giving other humans the power to dictate my actions by their approval or disapproval. Of course, I had long known that a large part of morality comes to us not from the heavens, but from our interactions with terrestrial authorities and peers. I had not appreciated that I was giving the role of the higher power to those here with me on earth. I think this revelation may have sparked my descent into disillusion, though I continue to cling on to Catholic identity today.

My personal faith journey has been a complex one. I stopped attending Mass regularly just over a year ago, although I have participated in Anglican Evensong services, as a member of my college choir. Until mid-February 2019, throughout my childhood, teenage years, and adult life so far, I attended Mass almost every Sunday. I lit candles and regularly blessed myself when passing churches, I silently said what little I remembered of the Angelus when I heard the bells ring out in public or before the Six One News.[1] I recited lengthy prayers practically every night, because I felt a guilty sensation if I did not. If someone was staying overnight at my house or I at theirs, I took care to bless myself in a slow, as-imperceptible-as-possible manner, for fear of being noticed and questioned or even laughed at. On the very rare occasion that I missed a night's prayers, I would repeat my normal routine a second time the following evening, or find some time during the day where I could steal away to a bathroom for a few minutes' praying privacy.

I am not trying to suggest any of this is common behaviour. I was recently diagnosed with Obsessive Compulsive Disorder, and I imagine there is a link between this and my pious practices. Following a particularly bad panic attack episode, I decided I would attempt to go a night without saying my prayers on purpose, to see how this might affect things.

I still identify as a Catholic in surveys and questionnaires, but recently I've become more uncertain. I believe God exists, but I'm not sure of all the details, and I'm not sure, somehow, if I really want to know. Maybe I don't need to. I'm happy to imagine different possibilities without hunkering down on one specific ideal of truth.

My faith has been shaken before. It was just as I reached the onset of puberty that I began seriously to question my sexual orientation. I wasn't ignorant of the apparent conflict between Abrahamic religions and 'homosexuals', but I wasn't sure where exactly the conservative argument stemmed from.

One night, I took my copy of the New Testament and searched for the passages where gay acts were seemingly discussed. I found it hard to understand. My experience of religion was based more in ritual and symbolism. My young mind was befuddled by instructions on the ethics of 'men laying with each other' and tales of Sodom and Gomorrah. I turned to the internet for help. Wikipedia informed me that Catholicism's issue was not with homosexual acts *per se*, but rather with any kind of intercourse without the express goal of procreation – and of course, such intercourse should take place inside marriage. I was taken aback, because the discussions of sex to which I had been exposed in pamphlets and puberty guides dealt more with anatomical details. Teenage girls' magazines had made it seem like any time you participated in any kind of act of a physical nature, you would instantaneously both become pregnant and contract a deadly disease. But all the sources of information I had encountered had stressed the importance of waiting until one was ready, of not giving into peer pressure. No one had ever suggested waiting until marriage. This was seemingly one of the core tenets of Catholicism – of Christianity, even – but neither Irish curriculum nor media had, to my memory, ever asked me to consider it.

Conclusion

As I've grown older, I've become more aware of the nuances of debate on such matters as sex, abortion, and the relationship between Scripture and its celebration. I've also discovered that much of the imagery I spent my young life venerating is dismissed as idolatry by many Protestant circles. Though I try to test my faith by reading criticism of my positions on doctrinal disputes, something within me still attributes an innate holiness to the trappings of Catholicism.

I once tried to discuss this with a peer who mocked my experience as indoctrination, which I hardly think is fair. I can accept the power of something while simultaneously questioning its authority. And, in spite of what some would-be iconoclasts might say, I think that Catholic ornamentation of biblical lessons has a valid purpose. Of course, the central value of anything is nested primarily in its essence, rather than its expression. But expression can colour our understanding of a phenomenon and lead us to appreciation of its merits and see a message we might not have otherwise considered. There are some passages in the Bible now that I cannot read without hearing a hymn which incorporates their words to resonate in my head, or picturing their representation in the form of lavish sculpture or painting. The passages have become all the more meaningful to me as a result.

After I stopped going to Mass every week, I mentioned this change to a secular friend, who responded that this was 'probably a good idea'. I'm used to irreligious peers looking down on Christian beliefs as regressive or ignorant. The disinclination among many young people to debate theology on a serious level has led me to refrain from 'outing' myself as a believer on many an occasion. It isn't worth the stares or the patronising diatribes. In the case of this particular Mass-related conversation, I think my friend was coming from a place of care and concern rather than condescension. I had told them some of my feelings of confusion and guilt relating to how I lived my life. But I think there was a slight misunderstanding on their part; I believe that those negative feelings are born from my interactions with other humans than those with God. Participating in and reflecting on religious rites can give me a sense of comfort that helps heal the anxiety provoked by fear of people's gossip and judgement.

Recently I have come to understand that my relationship with God is perhaps the one aspect of my life that is completely personal. I don't always find the inner workings of that relationship easy to understand, but I don't have to articulate them or justify it to anyone but myself.

Notes

1   RTÉ, or Raidió Teilifís Éireann, the Irish equivalent of the BBC, broadcasts the Angelus bells, accompanied by video clips of people in moments of calm and reflection, every evening at six pm. What would otherwise be the Six o'Clock News is therefore titled the Six One News, as it takes place at one-minute past six o'clock.

Does the Devil Have all the Best Tunes?

By Matthew Murphy

A beautiful Christianity does not have to be stale

Who doesn't like a surprise? Against the backdrop of a Western Christianity often synonymous with the word 'decline', anything which bucks the trend, not least concerning young people, is likely to grab headlines. It's perhaps all the more gratifying to learn that where young people *are* being drawn back to church, it's often within a rich tradition of liturgy, music and art that they are likely to find their spiritual home. Modern Christian worship, with its music echoing the latest chart hits and its venues at times resembling nightclubs, has been regarded by many commentators as being in a league with the very society – consumerist, individualistic, superficial, neoliberal – which young people, perhaps naturally, are yearning to escape, not least in their closest encounters with God.

The Washington Post recently reported on this trend, with the headline, 'Want millennials back in the pews? Stop trying to make church "cool"'. It argued that exercises in church rebranding and modernisation often had the potential to backfire among a generation of young people longing for more than mere entertainment, for a holistic, embodied and sacramental spirituality, for a sense of mystery, and for historical rootedness – or, as one commentator put it, for worship that is 'weird'. Another American news outlet reported that Evangelical megachurches were embracing liturgy to make worship more 'personal'; some were even beginning to order their worship around the liturgical calendar. Where do we draw the line between the expression and the essence of Christianity? Between belief and practice? Can Evangelicals be liturgical traditionalists? Needless to say, these questions are

99

nothing new: they sit in the very driving seat of Christianity's historical experience. Nowadays, for example, it is lost on few in the Anglican church that 'liberals' often tend to be most 'traditional' in their style of worship, and vice versa. There are reasons for this apparent contradiction which are almost self-apparent to most Christians, but less so to those – including my peers – outside the church. For many of them, anything which looks traditional on the outside, must be traditional and conservative on the inside.

I am a broad-church Christian: I practise within a specifically 'High Church' or 'Catholic' tradition (sometimes Anglican, sometimes Roman Catholic), about which I care very deeply. But I care as much about making my tradition serve the wider church and the world beyond, in a way that is as radical as it is authentic, and which speaks to truth. And so it is with some delight and hope that I read about young people who are shaking off generational stereotypes to find a style of worship that speaks authentically to them. Moreover, there are hints of a similar trend in Britain. One success story which is ostensibly youthful and Anglican in character was picked up by *The Times,* headlined thus: 'Why curious students put their faith in chapel visits'. It claimed that at Oxford, Cambridge and Durham universities, students are more than twice as likely to attend Sunday services as the wider population. A similar feature in the *Church Times* revealed that 'University chapels host a worshipping community of thousands'. It reported on a survey completed by 40 college chapels which indicated a Sunday attendance of 3000 people, of whom 46 per cent were students.

Does any of this matter? Two points are worth underscoring. Firstly, it won't come as much of a surprise to read that our ancient, elite universities are something of an exception in this respect; indeed, perhaps even an exception that proves the rule. Secondly, at face value, such reports might give some the impression of a chapel-going population drawn less directly to God and Christianity and more towards what some might regard as incidental, even extraneous, aspects of worship: the glorious music, the peace and tranquility, the arcane language, the liturgy, the art and the architecture – you might say, the expression of Christianity, rather than its essence. This perhaps explains the reluctance of the Church of England to include these figures within its overall tally for church attendance. Indeed, college chapels and cathedrals alike are often at pains to remind people that Choral Evensong, the liturgy which forms the bedrock of this tradition, is whatever you want to make of it: 'reflective'; 'a nice way to close the day'. Two statements in relation to rising attendances at cathedral services bear some of this out:

The breadth of this data is testimony to the wonderful diversity of cathedral activity. Some visitors are drawn to their ephemeral music and liturgy, some to their majestic architecture, some to learn about our rich heritage; others to mark life events, to come together as a civic community, and to visit one of the many creative installations to which only these lofty spaces can do full justice.[1]
The Third Church Estates Commissioner, Dr Eve Poole

Sir, with reference to your report "Stress drives workers to God" (Oct 24), whenever I visit cathedral cities, I try to attend evensong, but it won't please the Church of England to learn that it is because I find greater solace listening to the beautiful voices of the choristers — in a largely empty church, untainted by the faltering voices of a congregation singing hymns.[2]
A writer to *The Times*, October 2018

Likewise, in my experience as a director of an Oxford chapel choir, usually desperate for an audience on a Sunday evening, I was often falling over myself to tell my secularised peers that the chapel was welcoming to people of all beliefs and none, that it was basically a free concert, that we didn't actively evangelise, that we weren't directly affiliated with the Christian Union, and that copious amounts of alcohol would be served after the service.

I am inclined to welcome trends towards making spaces of worship more accessible and exciting. However, it can be easily inferred that this attractive cathedral, college chapel and choral tradition might not command the respect of the Christian community at large. The saying goes, 'the devil has the best tunes' – and so, hand-in-hand with the idols of aesthetics and music, is often a liberal theology preached from the chapel pulpit, a subdued or perhaps even non-existent evangelism, and a generous welcome to congregants of other faiths and none. I have witnessed firsthand the suspicion which this can draw from some religious conservatives, one of whom once told me that chapel did 'not count as church'. And now, working in the Church of England as an intern for a Bishop, as it grapples with questions of gender and sexuality, I am saddened by how deeply entrenched these so-called 'traditions' or 'camps' can be. The Reformation historian in me, on the one hand, thrives on a perpetual fascination with contemporary church politics; the Roman Catholic in me, on the other hand, finds it all quite exhausting. After all, although I subscribe to plenty of liberal theology, I would much rather not call myself a 'liberal'. And if *I* struggle with denominational politics, I can scarcely imagine how disorientated a newcomer to Christianity might feel.

I am proud of my church tradition. As an organist and choir director, I am especially proud of the rich and mature musicianship which it sustains. And I am thrilled that my peers in the young age bracket are drawn towards it. But I dislike seeing this tradition compartmentalised, exposing it to caricaturing by others. My fundamental concern is that if traditional or 'weird' liturgy becomes a form of momentary escapism for young people seeking to flee the world, or seeking to enter an idealised past for the sake of avoiding the gloomy present, it won't have staying power and won't speak to the world beyond the stained glass – it may become little more than a 'fad'. The trailblazing and radical clergyman Paul Oestreicher, lamenting the dearth of prophetic Christian leaders who can read the signs of the times, echoes some of my frustrations:

> If politics is about how we live together well or badly, it is disturbing how the average church congregation is sheltered from making the painful connection between the liturgy and the world of suffering – and its causes and consequences.[3]

In a similar vein of seeking to make sense of the relationship between Christianity and the world, but with a slightly different emphasis, Rowan Williams argues that:

> We need to think about a good deal more than just persuading European people back to Christian worship (though that would be a good start...).[4]

Therefore, the Christian impulse to be critical of the world, and to regard our place within it as transient, should not invite a religious practice where we can shop around for whatever form of worship or liturgy enables us to most successfully disconnect ourselves from the world, nor should it preclude our ability to engage with the world and to shape it. Admittedly, I have encountered some terrific and world-aware preaching in my college chapel and in other sites of traditional worship, such as cathedrals. The discourse is often humane and well-tempered, without being feeble; radical without being fundamentalist. Indeed, my own college in Oxford contributed more than its fair share to the flourishing of a moderate sixteenth-century Christian humanism; Erasmus himself spoke highly of the college; perhaps he sat in the same very chapel. I would like to think that his ideas might resonate with our contemporary social and political struggles. Later in the century, the eminent theologian Richard Hooker, whose ideas have done more than most to sustain my love affair with Anglicanism, established himself as a fellow at my college and helped to devise a consensus for a fractured Church of England, still very much riding the waves of the Reformation. Today, my chapel welcomes speakers from a range of church backgrounds, and not just clergy: we've had journalists, artists, and aid workers. Moreover, since the chapel unashamedly seeks to be a place open to people of all faiths and none, those who preach therein must endeavour, in some way, to deliver the Christian message in a way that makes sense to the wider world. It is, in my view, a powerful form of evangelism, without the heavy emphasis on personal salvation which, ultimately, turns many people off.

Nevertheless, it's hard to escape the fact that tradition, liturgy, and especially music, is at the core of what makes this form of worship attractive to so many people. But do we stop there? How do we ensure that it doesn't become an end in itself, but rather, in the words of Williams, is a good place to *start*? Britain has a vibrant and widely-cherished choral tradition, and sacred choral music is more compelling and powerful than ever – yet, statistically speaking, we are one of the world's most irreligious societies. I'm not sure that this is entirely a coincidence. In some sectors our choral tradition is too sanitised, too proud of its own cultural idiosyncrasy, sometimes downright elitist. This is both a reality and a matter of perception. Our great cathedrals and choral foundations inspire much awe and admiration, but the tradition at large could do more to inspire participation.

In some ways, the 'traditional' expression of Christian worship which appeals to some young people, as described, runs the risk of being cast within the same paradigm as modern worship styles with which it supposedly competes: as one of many expressions of Christianity, all vying for supremacy among the young consumer base within the crowded religious marketplace. Indeed, it is not especially surprising that most reports on these trends hark from the United States, where the church's outward manifestation as a marketplace of traditions is fairly well embedded, for reasons which don't need spelling out. It is an ecclesiological model which, in the grand scheme of things, is far from traditional or historically-rooted in itself. By this measure, modern worship and traditional liturgy are seen as equal and opposite and directly comparable, when in reality they fulfil their functions very differently, draw upon different theologies and are often built upon considerably different ecclesiologies. In the Church of England, the distinction between 'High Church' and 'Low Church' is one which implies that the church is simply a stylistic spectrum, with little regard for the fact that sacramental liturgy and word-centred worship work in functionally diverse ways and can represent profoundly different ways of relating to God. This in turn explains my earlier observation of young people outside the church not being able to fully grasp why a modern, 'happy-clappy' church might be conservative, even fundamentalist.

It is a particular form of secularism which has, in a sense, brought this about – commodifying styles of worship and relegating religion to a matter of private interest and consumption. In reality, most religious traditions are suffocated when forced into the private sphere, which in turn breeds resistance and fundamentalism in a way that is often self-fulfilling. The point is that if the character of a religion and the extent of its appeal is determined by its outward expression, then we may well have missed the point. The customer is not always right. A recent blog post spoke to this theme, suggesting that the Church of England's solutions for becoming more 'relevant' to young people are 'always couched in terms of presentation and polish – never in terms of substance,' in 'a superficial commitment to loud music, beautifully presented videos and incessantly, ludicrously, smiling people, who appear to be the models for 1980s action figures.' The writer points out that for the church to be 'relevant', it would do better to tone down on the optimism and focus on what is wrong with the world.[5] There is a complex theology at play here – which would very quickly have us talking about Augustine, no doubt – but that's the point: we ought to be talking about ideas too.

My conviction, however, is that art and music in the Christian context have the capacity to directly connect with these ideas; to help build a bridge between theory and practice. The arts are already doing this, to a great extent – it just needs exposing: which is my intent in the forthcoming words. There is a reservoir of talent, creativity and passion at the heart of the church which has the potential to draw young people of all backgrounds to the church, but also to draw them back out to the world equipped with a better understanding of Christian teaching, a sense of the church being alive and kicking rather than stuck in a time warp, and a willingness to engage constructively with other faiths. That's because music and art hold the key to unlocking vast swathes of theology, eschatology and social teaching for young people in a way that is accessible, but also challenging and not necessarily straightforward. Music – in composing, listening and performing – has the power to transport us beyond ourselves: towards the divine. But it also provokes us to become more in touch *with* ourselves: towards in the human. Music, art and liturgy, for all its beauty and seeming perfection, sits at the intersection of the popular and the elitist, the secular and the sacred, and the human and the divine. It has, as we have seen, been bringing young people into contact with Christianity; it could encourage even more. And its connective power can help to bring Christianity and its rich traditions back into contact with the world.

Pulling out all the stops

It strikes me that many religious testimonials (usually by Christian evangelicals) begin with: 'I was raised a Catholic' – and the rest is history. I am somewhat similar. Specifically, it was a diet of lukewarm Irish Catholicism which I was fed growing up in Enniskillen, County Fermanagh. When I took up the organ and singing at the age of 16, it was perhaps inevitable that I would quickly become frustrated with my church's neglect of a monumental music tradition to which it could lay claim, appalled by the way the Second Vatican Council seemed to have vandalised it. I tried my best to wage a traditionalising crusade within my parish church's music department, and encountered some fairly stiff resistance from some of the clergy I worked with. I was probably a bit of a snob about it all.

Ironically, my eagerness to revive what I saw as a historically-rooted, beautiful and full-blooded Catholic liturgy brought me closer to Protestantism (well, actually Anglicanism, but Northern Ireland has no time for such fine distinctions!). Several of its characteristics appealed to me: the rich and cherished tradition of hymn singing, the enthusiastic participation of the congregation in the singing (Catholics are famously reluctant to do likewise) and the centrality of the organist and organ music to worship. My other consideration was that most Anglican churches in Ireland, as in England, are actually older than most Roman Catholic churches, for obvious historical reasons – indeed, many Anglican churches started off as 'Catholic' churches – therefore, with another dose of irony, giving me a greater sense of historical rootedness. From a purely aesthetic perspective, many Anglican churches have matured over the centuries, their dull outer stonework blending in with the landscape – perhaps what Winston Churchill had in mind when he spoke of the 'dreary steeples of Fermanagh and Tyrone' in February 1922. Their Roman Catholic counterparts, on the other hand, are ornate, at times extravagant, you might even say kitsch, if particularly unsympathetic, built in a relatively new neo-gothic or modernist style, with a sanctuary remodelled – often rather distastefully – in the 1970s to accommodate the reforms of the Second Vatican Council.

However, I take some satisfaction from the fact that my teenage denominational meanderings were driven by more than aesthetic concerns. In general, I was hungry for a Christianity that was punchier and a bit more self-assured – or, at the very least, I was determined to prove that the severe religious and political labels foisted upon everyone in Northern Ireland at birth were fickle and could be easily transcended – and yes, I also flirted with unionist politics! On a mission to make more sense of Protestantism, I set out to make friends with Protestants and to read the Bible, frustrated by my rudimentary knowledge of the text. Diametrically opposed to my aesthetic and musical considerations, you might say, was this longing for a religion that was articulate and that could explain itself. I didn't mind Catholic sacramentalism, but it did frustrate me that many Catholics – clergy included – didn't seem able to explain why they performed these rituals. It all smacked of 'going through the motions'. Hardly the first time Catholicism had been thus characterised!

I eventually went to Oxford as an Organ Scholar and history student. It was the ideal combination – the two aspects of my university career were mutually enriching. I felt incredibly fortunate that after only a few years on the organ, I had managed to land myself right at the heart of one of the best places in the world to do choral and organ music. As a relative newcomer and outsider to the tradition, I was impressed by the degree of passion and commitment among young people – admittedly, usually from highly privileged backgrounds – for making music to a high standard in a liturgical context.

The college chapel tradition where I directed a choir was attractive for many reasons, not least for all the aesthetic pleasantries and the insightful preaching to which I referred in the introduction, above. More than that, the liturgy – and Choral Evensong in particular – seemed to marry my ostensibly competing desires for a form of worship that is pleasing on the eye and on the ear, and one that is articulate. Indeed, most people will agree that what makes Evensong so captivating, besides the music, is that the words of the King James Bible and Prayer Book liturgy are themselves beautiful, reverent, and otherworldly. And these words are given new dimensions in the singing of psalms, anthems, hymns and canticles.

However, I would be the first to admit that, in my work as a choir director, I often feel like a marketing manager too. It is a condition exacerbated in the Oxford scenario where approximately 25 college chapels, which all do broadly similar things, are crying out for attention – indeed, it is a religious marketplace like no other. It is a sense which has been especially acute in the context of lockdown and the church's growing presence in the virtual world, where I've been under pressure to produce high quality video material, more sophisticated and more interesting than the college next door. With most churches filling the online space, we live in a truly universalised religious marketplace. A recent report in *The Guardian* observed that 'Mass hoppers' and assessments of viewing figures during the Covid pandemic were fuelling pressure and anxiety among Catholic priests in Ireland. And so, fundamentally, as someone whose first and automatic loyalty has always been to his parish church or college chapel, the idea that I might 'shop around' for the right church felt absurd. In a sense, I've been extremely fortunate that in Oxford, both my college chapel and my parish church (the University Church of St Mary the Virgin), perhaps predictably, were compatible with my tastes – theologically, aesthetically and musically. Moreover, being loyal to a parish in itself guarantees a broadly similar form and style of worship.

And yet, to be loyal to one's parish also implies a degree of allegiance which supersedes or transcends the purely aesthetic and stylistic; it suggests a longing to be rooted at the heart of a local community, both horizontally with those around us and vertically with the generations who, for centuries, worshipped God on the same spot. I'd like to think that, in principle, if I ever found myself in a town or village with a parish church that was evangelical or 'low church' in its leanings, I would establish myself there nonetheless – although I have yet to be confronted with such a scenario. More to the point, I've been fortunate to have spent most of my life in countries where a stable parish structure exists – either in predominantly Catholic Ireland or Chile (from where my mother hails) or in the Church of England. A brief spell in the United States, as you might expect, had me totally disorientated to begin with: God was spoken of everywhere, and was everywhere to be seen, and yet, to my Western European eyes, the church was nowhere to be found. This takes me back to my issue with Christianity – especially as manifested in the United States – as a religious marketplace, and of a church and a press which obsesses with 'what young people want', often in terms of form, aesthetics and music.

In this brief summary of my personal journey, I hope I've left the impression of a teenage self preoccupied with the frivolities, you might say, of liturgy, sacred music and aesthetics, and who, to some extent, let those considerations determine his allegiances. This was, in part, fuelled by the particular Northern Irish context in which every outwardly distinguishing aspect of religiosity, culture and identity is more pronounced than ever – from musical traditions right down to what people wear to church on a Sunday. The Catholic church I attended in Enniskillen as a child sits directly opposite an Anglican church, and so, standing outside the church (or 'the chapel', as Catholic churches in Northern Ireland are typically referred to) on a Sunday morning, watching the smartly dressed Protestants make their way to church while my father made idle chit-chat,

I could not help but draw stark comparisons. As I learnt more about Christianity, especially through history, the flood gates opened to everything else that mattered – what a church thinks and teaches, how a church is governed and structured, where it stands in relation to society. When I realised that I was gay, some of these questions were thrown into even sharper relief. The early modern period has a lot to teach us about the debates which can be had over *adiaphora* – matters in the expression of Christianity (such as church governance and style of worship) which are not essential to faith or salvation, but are perhaps no less important by other metrics.

And so, while remaining wholeheartedly committed to my work as a church musician, and most comfortable within a High Church tradition, I'd like to think that I'm not quite as fickle as *The Washington Post* (see headline above) or some churches themselves would make me or my peers out to be. The way a church conducts itself liturgically, aesthetically or musically is but one strand of what determines my allegiance – and even then, it informs only one *level* of allegiance, and quite a low one at that: as a Christian, my ultimate allegiance is to God. Above, I referred to my practising within a 'specifically Catholic' tradition, which, of course, is something of an oxymoron. The specifics are in some of the stylistic externalities which I've talked about – but my Catholicism, if being true to itself, is about more than an affinity for a particular style. It is, almost by definition, about how I understand the church to exist and be organised on a global scale, about social teaching, and so on. If we think of Catholicism's 'bells and smells' as simply a matter of style, then we reduce them to frivolities (which you might reasonably, after careful consideration, think they are), and we fundamentally misunderstand Catholicism. Likewise, my Anglicanism is about much more than my love for Evensong and the choral tradition: it's about ideas I have on the relationship between church and state; it's about the Hookerian coalition of scripture, tradition and reason. And yet, these wider concerns are not inaccessible to engagement and communication with the world of art and music: the interior must always be in contact with the exterior. I would like for the church's tradition of art and music, therefore, to serve all the other ideas that I and my peers have in relation to theology and the role of the church in the world, in ways that are meaningful and even radical.

Escaping escapism

There is a notion of perfection and sublimity attached to choral music as performed within the Anglican tradition which explains its appeal among (some) young people and foreign tourists alike, flocking as they do to King's College Chapel, Cambridge. I can't deny the fundamental human impulse to seek divine transcendence within a tradition that is complete and makes sense to itself. Nor can I deny, as a Christian, that there is obviously something more than human at play here. I also can't deny the fundamental Christian impulse to retreat from the world, and to encounter God in a special way through the sacraments. However, if some of these impulses are merely compartmentalised and satisfied within a weekly act of worship, then perhaps we risk a trivialisation of transcendence, a Christian escapism, an exercise in self-gratification, a Christianity which exists as a relic of the past, perhaps even – in the words of N. T. Wright – an 'aesthetic pornography'. Christianity – or even spirituality, more broadly – if it is being true to itself, should not be a panacea, giving us what we want, on demand. And within this religious context, the best art and music must, at times, be simple and austere, challenging, even unsettling, while pointing us towards something perfect, mysterious and so much greater than ourselves. This would give music and the arts the power to engage young people with the church more meaningfully and broadly than ever. We can set music and the arts at the centre of the church's mission within a broken world.

I'm not suggesting that we take an iconoclastic axe to timeless liturgical practices, art and music. I'm not suggesting that liturgy needs to rebrand: liturgy does not need to sell itself. But if young people – Christians, non-Christians, and everyone in between – are indeed being drawn towards traditional worship in a search for historical rootedness, we would do well to remind ourselves that 'root', from the Latin *radix*, gives birth to the word 'radical'. Music and the arts, situated as they are at the intersection of the human and the divine, have the capacity to express this kind of radicalism in secular and sacred contexts.

More like a building site than a monument

The popular and the elite

In many ways, a radical and groundbreaking streak is already present in high liturgy and the choral tradition, it just needs to be spelt out. The words above, by Daniel T. Jenkins – 'more like a building site than a monument' – describe, perhaps in more reformed than Catholic terms, one way of seeing the visible church as it exists on earth, through time.[6] They resonate with the historical dynamism and creativity of the Christian liturgical and artistic tradition. To begin with, as my college chaplain never tires of reminding us, the office of Evensong was the brainchild of a religious radical of his own time: Archbishop of Canterbury, Thomas Cranmer, who steered Henry VIII's break with Rome in his own theologically reformist direction. He overhauled the vastly complicated liturgical menu of medieval England, merging the evening offering of Vespers and Compline into the simple office of Evening Prayer – or 'Evensong', as it became known. Crucially, the English text which he devised for the liturgy, arcane and obscure to our ears, was then a radical departure from the conventional Latin.

The tension between the popular and the elite is never far from the surface in any narrative of liturgical reform. Even distinguished historians have struggled to reach a consensus on the matter in respect of the English Reformation, some lauding the replacement of a labyrinth of liturgical intricacies with a streamlined and accessible structure of worship which inspired *common* prayer – hence the Book – and others noting that, for a largely illiterate population with a strong affinity for traditional piety, a revised liturgical textbook and a Bible translation made little difference, it may even have been alienating.

'Popular' and 'elite' tendencies also jostle for supremacy in the musical and choral tradition which has established itself at the heart of Evening Prayer. Psalm-singing, nowadays typically performed by the choir to the steady and mesmerising rhythm of Anglican chant, actually formed the bedrock of congregational singing among early evangelical movements in Europe – and Cromwell's New Model Army, Puritan in its instincts, went into battle with psalms on the their lips. Likewise, hymn-singing – much of which grew out of psalm-singing – was a popular pursuit, but it was the nineteenth-century Oxford Movement, Catholic in its instincts, which helped to find a definitive place for hymn singing within the Anglican service. Today, the nation's favourite hymn, 'Jerusalem', is not strictly a hymn at all, since it isn't a prayer to God. Moreover, its contemporary characterisation as middle England's anthem hardly speaks to its radical and anti-establishment roots.

Christmas

Christmas itself is an interesting phenomenon within this context. The Festival of Nine Lessons and Carols, beamed across the world from King's Cambridge on Christmas Eve, grew out of a widespread nineteenth-century tradition of performing carols – generally considered to be secular and largely excluded from Christian worship – at people's houses and in pubs, followed by the Bishop of Truro's attempt to bring this drunken revelry under control and feed it into the sanitised environment of the church and an ordered liturgy. If, in today's world, more people are singing *Guide me, O thou great Jehovah* at Welsh rugby matches than in churches, what is the Bishop of Llandaff going to do about it?

Today, I often wonder whether extravagant festive choral offerings and liturgies might be interpreted as missing the point of Christmas: that of the incarnation, and of Christ's birth in the most humble and precarious of circumstances, even if so many of our carols (Away in a Manger; Infant Holy, Infant Lowly) so perfectly encapsulate the Christ-child's humble and earthly presence. Sometimes I think that we are like the Magi approaching the infant Christ in the stable: self-conscious enough to know that our rich offerings and human pretences to power pale in comparison with the Christ-child, no less the Prince of Peace, no less the God incarnate. It is what makes the story all the more mysterious, and yet no less real. Sometimes, potent ironies like these are the best way of getting a point across.

Music lists

The choral tradition is countercultural by the standards of the modern Western world, but to the tourist queueing for Evensong at King's Cambridge, it is an unashamedly English and Anglican cultural expression. And yet, it owes so much of its hymnody to Methodists and Lutherans, who in turn owe many of their hymns to secular folk tunes. Moreover, much of England's choral repertoire comes from continental European composers of Renaissance polyphony. Therefore, the tradition is by no means specifically British, let alone English. The connections with Germany – through Handel, J. S. Bach, Samuel Wesley and so on – are well documented. As a choir director in my college chapel, there was an approach to designing music lists which was almost promiscuous as to style, country of origin or denominational background. For some, I understand, this kind of Anglican fudge might prove unsatisfactory – but this kind of variety was enriching and satisfying to my own ecumenical aspirations. And that's before one begins to pry the complicated spirituality of many of our staple composers, many of whom were/are far from unswerving in their beliefs:

> *I am friend, fellow traveller, and agnostic supporter of the Christian faith.*
> John Rutter

> *There is no reason why an atheist could not write a good Mass.*
> Ralph Vaughan Williams

> *He was never more than an agnostic who veered toward belief.*
> Ursula Howells, on her husband Herbert Howells

Naturally, the profiles of some of these composers could easily feed the view that the arts can lead people away from religion, or that aesthetics can become a religion in itself. It is a philosophical trajectory which lends itself to the narrative of James Joyce's 'Künstlerroman' ('artist's novel'), *A Portrait of the Artist as a Young Man,* published in 1916. It follows the intellectual awakening of a young Irishman, Stephen Dedalus, as he drifts from a deep Catholic religiosity towards a philosophical aestheticism. He concludes that Ireland, with its restrictive Catholic and nationalist conventions, does not allow him to express himself fully as an artist – and so he leaves for Europe. And yet, as much as we like to probe our great musicians and artists for their obscure spiritualities, their agnosticism, or their philosophical aestheticism, a generous interpretation would still put them much closer to God – or at least to a comprehensive understanding of Christianity – than most of modern Britain.

Dynamic tradition: Christian arts and crisis

Unsympathetic readers among you might say that I've spoiled something special which is what tends to happen when religious tradition comes under the historian's, or the anthropologist's, or the sociologist's, microscope. You might even say that I'm peddling the view that all religion is invented. And yet, it is in the nature of Christianity to question what we take for granted, to decode and to affirm that appearances can be deceptive – but without always dismantling certainties. From the point of view of young people engaging with the church, especially through music and the arts, and for the sake of religion itself, there is a value in unearthing the dynamism of tradition. The arts often provide the fullest expression of this dynamism, since they form the core of our human input to the sacred and divine. If it is true that 'plus ça change, plus c'est la même chose' (the more things change, the more they stay the same), then what have we to fear?

That so much Christian art and music can be outpoured in a time of crisis is a powerful testimony to its dynamism. The trauma of the Reformation, on the one hand, provoked the devastating destruction of swathes of medieval Europe's musical fabric. And I cannot even begin my attempt to situate the arts at the heart of the church's mission without acknowledging that art and Christianity – to say nothing of Islam – can often be uncomfortable bedfellows; at times directly opposed. It is a tension which has resulted in iconoclasm and in some of the greatest outbursts of violence ever carried out in the name of God. But the Reformation, at least indirectly, perhaps unintentionally, inspired no shortage of creativity, and musical innovation was broadly acceptable among new Protestants and Counter-Reformation Catholics alike: indeed, the story goes that Palestrina, fearing the Council of Trent's ban of polyphony, composed his *Missa Papae Marcelli* especially for the council delegates to demonstrate that it was perfectly possible to write polyphony with words that could be clearly understood, but which was no less pleasing to the ear. I think he was right.

My understanding of music and art which comes out of crisis takes me from sixteenth-century Trento to modern-day Coventry, where I currently find myself employed as a Bishop's assistant. In November 1940, the city was largely destroyed in a 'blitz' carried out by the Luftwaffe. Among the casualties was the medieval cathedral, mostly reduced to rubble, with the exception of the tower and the outer walls. A new cathedral, built in a striking modernist style, sits adjacent to the ruins. It has captivated me, albeit slowly – perhaps the way any good piece of art should. The cathedral is itself a work of art, and contains within it some spectacular individual pieces – chief among them Graham Sutherland's tapestry *Christ in Glory in the Tetramorph,* one of the world's largest, and John Piper and Patrick Reyntiens's Baptistry Window. The cathedral is authentic in its modernity and modernism: a symbol of hope, renewal and resurrection. Its art speaks directly to its mission as a centre for reconciliation: indeed, that an entirely new cathedral should be built, rather than a restoration of the ruins, was considered to be fundamental to its reconciling mission. And yet, the new structure echoes the past, speaks to the present and anticipates the future, all at once. The outcome is, in the words of its architect Sir Basil Spence, an 'alchemy of art and architecture', which contains 'understandable beauty to help the ordinary man to worship with sincerity.'

In tandem with this outpouring of visual creativity, Benjamin Britten was commissioned to write the *War Requiem,* which was premiered in the cathedral in 1962. The work poignantly juxtaposes the traditional words of the Latin Mass with nine poems by Wilfred Owen, who was angry that Christianity had betrayed its own pacifist ethic, and its premiere saw solos performed by a British tenor, a German baritone and a Russian soprano. It is as challenging for the listener as it is for the performer. Britten himself was a determined pacifist, an agnostic at most, but no less a humanist admirer of Christian ethics.

Ostensibly a world away from the aesthetic pleasures of my sixteenth-century Oxford college chapel, the art and architecture of Coventry Cathedral perhaps comes closest to expressing my aspiration for the role of the arts in a dynamic and outward-looking church with which young people can meaningfully engage – not least because there is a rich diversity of backgrounds and identities represented among the cathedral's young choristers. It offers an example of how the arts can be a vehicle for change and a powerful response to moments of crisis; to Christians like me it is proof that the Holy Spirit is at work, breathing life into tradition. That the church – metaphorically and often literally – is a building site, shouldn't diminish its hold on our consciences and our senses. At the very least, it doesn't stop Barcelona's Sagrada Familia – over a century in the building – from being one of Europe's most visited tourist sites. If anything, my sense is that its status as an almost perpetual building site, as a work in progress, is part of what makes it inspire such fascination and curiosity. In this respect, neither Coventry Cathedral nor the Sagrada Familia are instantly gratifying in every aspect of their aesthetic quality – but they are no less impressive for that.

Urbi et orbi – to the city and to the world

The arts in the context of liturgy and worship have power, not just in being aesthetically compelling, but also in how they simultaneously reflect the human and the divine, that essential dichotomy which lies at the heart of the Christian story. But what if we turn our attention to the secular sphere? Or what if a global pandemic were to strike which might deny us access to our church buildings? Ben Quash, writing on the seventeenth-century poet Henry Vaughan, who was something of a religious exile in Puritan England, observes that 'Vaughan was forced to cope with attachment to a denomination denied its public ceremonies and ordinances, yet one of the consequences of this trauma was a stimulus to searching, reflection and enquiry after God in unwonted places.'[7] What might this mean for today's church musicians or artists?

A theology for the arts

What does the modern-day Christian do with a secular society as obsessed with classical and choral music as Britain? Or with a country like Estonia, one of the world's least religious countries, but with a famously well-established folk and choral singing tradition? What do we do with a Mozart Mass setting, perhaps too frivolous or sensual for a liturgical context, but nonetheless an impressive piece of music? How do we speak to the universality of music in every culture, civilisation, and era? George Corbett writes that 'classical music's divorce from God has been one of the great failures of our times.' How might we repair the damage?

We could remind people just how much our musical heritage owes to the Judeo-Christian tradition. We could draw people's attention to the profound religiosity of many of our great composers – like Olivier Messiaen, or indeed Arvo Pärt, himself an Estonian – and to the fact that even those who declared themselves to be atheist or agnostic, such as Vaughan Williams, Brahms, Berlioz and Verdi, were nonetheless sympathetic to Christianity in a way that would be unimaginable in the severe secularism of our contemporary world, where you are either for religion or against it.

But religion, and Christianity more specifically, isn't just there in the roots of our musical heritage, or even just in its power to transport us to some kind of ill-defined mystical dimension. Theology, some argue, sits at the heart of the very music itself – in its tensions and resolutions, its form and structure, its tonality, its rhythm, its improvisations – in the very dots on the manuscript. Professor Jeremy Begbie, of Duke University, has illustrated this most prolifically at an academic level.[8] He is particularly keen to remind his readers that in music, as opposed to visual art, the way in which we can hear different sounds as distinct but also together, within our entire auditory 'frame', is a good way of making sense of the doctrine of the Trinity, for instance. In doing so he succeeds a line of classical philosophers and church fathers who thought about the metaphysics of music, and especially harmony, and the way it could give expression to the cosmic order. Augustine explored this in *De Musica,* believing that it offered humans an insight into the created order, and into God himself. If Palestrina was convinced that beautiful and elaborate choral music would not obscure the message of the text, he might also have been relieved to know that even a wordless music could be as effective in pointing us towards God.

The arts as a social building-block

Therefore, for all the spiritual ambiguity of many great composers, music's inherent theological quality can ultimately transcend the individual and point towards a greater truth, towards something bigger than our individual selves. Engaging with music is an instinct common to all of humanity, and therefore it holds the potential to promote mutual understanding among cultures, nationalities and faiths, while cultivating a sense of a common good which currently is being lost to some of the worst excesses of our contemporary politics. The Roman poet Terence famously said *Homo sum, humani nihil a me alienum puto* – 'I am human, and I think nothing human is alien to me.' With the help of the arts, common as they are to all of us, might not these enlightened words help to bring us out of our trenches?

What if, therefore, churches practised ecumenical engagement more widely through music and choirs? We might, for instance, draw inspiration from the Revd Donald Reeves, who has spent over a decade peace-building in the Balkans, and describes how he has been emboldened in his work by his experience as an organist playing the music of J. S. Bach. Reeves worked tirelessly to promote Muslim-Christian collaboration in Bosnia, and now works to bring together Orthodox Serbs and Kosovo Albanians. All the while he has persisted with Bach's Leipzig Chorales, and describes how 'the music, like a mirror, reflects back with some clarity that hope which is essential in the long and difficult processes of bringing former enemies together.' How might these ideas help to alleviate the situation in such places as Nagorno-Karabakh?

I have experienced the power of music and art as a tool for interfaith and intercultural exchange in Northern Ireland in both secular and religious contexts. More broadly, as someone who has spent too much time veering all over the place from one Christian church to another, I have found that music has helped me to root myself within the diverse landscape of religion, and has given me a universal language with which to communicate with those representing other traditions. Every faith tradition, even those which reject the arts, nonetheless has a relationship with the arts and a set of ideas which guides this relationship – and this is usually a useful entry point for making sense of a wider belief system. It was the twentieth-century English poet Donald Davie, for example, who asserted that, contrary to widely-held stereotypes, there was such a thing as a Protestant Calvinist aesthetic which expressed the virtues of simplicity, sobriety and measure. In musical terms, we should also say that silence matters as much as sound; indeed, one of the first lessons in organ playing is that the space between the notes is as important as the notes themselves. And, as an organist starting out in the Anglican tradition, it seemed as though every single movement during the service had to be covered by some kind of music – the Catholic church, for all its flaws, was at least comfortable with silence. In sum, an appreciation of religious art, of its presence and absence within different traditions, is ideal ground upon which to build an understanding of a complicated religious landscape.

The very act of making music, both corporately and individually, also discloses some clues about how we might reimagine society and successfully co-exist as humans. It is very hard – nigh on impossible – to profoundly dislike someone after having successfully collaborated in music. Yes, corporate music-making can also be frustrating, and 'enemies' can be made along the way – but this reflects the fundamental humanity of our endeavour, and therefore anyone watching something as divine as Carols from King's ought to think, 'I can do that too', because even the best choirs experience bumps along the road. On a deeper level, the tediousness, discipline, and even misery of rehearsing, perhaps with people you don't instinctively get along with, has a lot to teach us about what it means to be free. David Brooks and Jonathan Sacks both evoke the image of piano practice to elucidate Locke's distinction between liberty (freedom *to* do things which implies a degree of responsibility) and licence (freedom *from* constraint, to do whatever one pleases).[9] Real practice involves discipline, responsibility and constraint. The result, however, can be liberating: freedom *to* play music effortlessly, freedom *to* live in peace with those who disagree with us, and so on. It is no secret that Sacks, in using this illustration, was a strong supporter of a collective liberty which is facilitated by constraint and responsibility – and it is no secret that this view is far from universally popular, not least among the younger generation. And yet, this message has been at the heart of our response to the coronavirus pandemic: lockdown now, freedom later. It will surely be part of our response to even greater threats, like the climate crisis. It also lies at the core of what it means to lead a Christian life and to fulfil the common good: the idea that a certain degree of sacrifice and constraint can actually be liberating, enriching and life-giving in the long-term.

That being said, on a deeper level, art can also draw us in the opposite direction: away from a universalist, 'all-seeing' manifestation of secularism which reduces our actions as humans to instrumentalist, managerial and functional decisions based on negotiations of interest. That's because, as Rowan Williams points out, the very existence of art implies the existence of what he calls 'inaccessible perspectives' which are profoundly and necessarily non-secular in character, since the non-secular, as he understands it, is 'a willingness to see things or other persons as the objects of another sensibility than my own.' Secularism, by comparison, sees 'nothing beyond the processes of successful negotiation', or, 'no substantive truth but a series of contests about sustainable control and the balances of power.' In other words, art is special because our awareness of it is partly defined by an external awareness of how others see or hear it, therefore inviting a variety of seeings, readings and hearings which we can be aware of and attentive to, but which are no less inaccessible to us as subjects. Translated into the moral sphere, he borrows Raimond Gaita's example of how 'one of the quickest ways to make prisoners morally invisible to their guards is to deny them visits from their loved ones, thereby, ensuring that the guards never see them through the eyes of those who love them.'[10] And so the arts have a lot to teach us about a world of different perspectives and moral relations, something which a certain kind of secularism cannot. The power of the arts to help us make sense of our common humanity therefore meets its limit, but also its fulfilment, in the existence of perspectives which we can imagine, but cannot fully access. It is the difference between 'visualising' and 'seeing'. To paraphrase Williams, there is no vantage point on this earth that leaves no room for any seeing from elsewhere. There are limits, therefore, to use of the arts as a 'common currency' for understanding each other – not least in the world of religion, where talk of 'common currency' invokes the image of the superficial religious marketplace. Nonetheless, these are necessary and useful limits, in helping us to navigate the relationship between identities, between plurality and homogeneity, between the subject and the object, and in equipping us with the capacity to 'imaginatively construct' inaccessible perspectives and to sense the variety of readings, seeings and hearings that make up the world.

We perhaps do not give my generation enough credit for making sense of these boundaries through their political struggles. From the climate crisis to Black Lives Matter, young people are forever navigating the frontier between common concerns and distinct injustices, sometimes with more success than others. My generation is leading the charge against many of these evils of the modern world which are pushing ever greater numbers of us into war, climate injustice, famine and financial crisis, attentive to how common problems interact with specific situations and perspectives. My own youthful idealism – or what's left of it – is convinced that the arts have more than a merely peripheral role to play in this context, both directly and indirectly. The arts and music are perfectly placed to help mediate tensions which exist within our church and in wider society – between secular and sacred, human and divine, old and new, individual and social. The arts can be at the core of the church's mission to make disciples but also to promote goodwill and understanding with those who don't identify as Christians. The arts can also be at the core of our public policy, at the centre of how we plan for rapidly increasing urbanisation in the developing world and how to respond to fragmented and polarised societies in the Western world. I'm not naive to the fact that a state's power to connect with people's emotions through the arts can be extremely dangerous – consider, for example, how the Nazis used Wagner's music to their ends. But used wisely and sensitively, the arts can do tremendous good.

Which takes me back to where I started. If we say that young people who are drawn to a Christian worship that is rich in art and music are simply longing for a momentary, otherworldly escape from the troubles of society, then we fundamentally underestimate the power of sacred art and music to speak to the human and the divine simultaneously, to be both reassuring and challenging, to illuminate a mysterious God and a complicated world, and to reconcile how things are, with how things would, could or should be. We also underestimate the power of the arts to further the aims of the church beyond the liturgy, and to further those aims which it shares with the wider world, and with other faiths. At the heart of a church tradition that is ostensibly old-fashioned, even stale, is a medium for creativity, which is a concept that can speak to us theologically in more ways than we might think. Once again, Rowan Williams makes a lucid observation on this point:

> When we see our souls as called to create because they come from the hand of a creator, as creative in the degree that they are aligned with a mysterious and indestructible loving purpose, we have something of immeasurable value to inform and sustain our culture.[11]

Therefore, the liturgical, aesthetic and musical tradition which could fall into the trap of being regarded as self-serving, too culturally embedded, concerned with 'keeping up appearances', can be vibrant, exciting, progressive, transformational, and God-centred. And so, the arts – with the church as their pioneer and purveyor – can be part of the bridge which links a young person's desire for a moment in the otherworld, to their desire to be part of a movement for another world.

Notes

1   'Cathedral attendance rose by three per cent last Christmas,' *The Church Times,* 24th October, 2018.

2   'Letters to the Editor,' *The Times,* 25th October, 2018.

3   'Our age needs prophets. Where have they gone?' *The Church Times,* 29th July, 2016.

4   R. Williams, *Faith in the public square* (London, 2012), p. 73.

5   C. Bell, 'Church of England: Will the Quest to be Woke Save Us?', *ViaMedia.News,* 16th January, 2021.

6   D. T. Jenkins, 'A Protestant aesthetic? A conversation with Donald Davie' in *The Journal of the United Reformed Church History Society,* 3/9 (October, 1986), p. 371.

7   B. Quash, *Found Theology: History, Imagination and the Holy Spirit* (London, 2013), p. 193.

8   J. Begbie, *Resounding truth: Christian wisdom in the world of music* (Michigan, 2007).

9   J. Sacks, *Morality: Restoring the common good in divided times* (London, 2020).

10 Williams, *Faith in the public square,* pp. 13–17.

11 Williams, *Faith in the public square,* p. 74.

Religion and the Environment

By Connie Tongue

'God loans all of creation to humankind for our use: the high, the low, everything. If we misuse this privilege, God's Justice gives creation permission to offer Humankind a reminder.' These words of the twelfth-century 'rebel' nun Hildegard von Bingen may be separated from us by almost a thousand years, yet when read in the current context they lose none of their power. As the forces of nature become increasingly unpredictable it seems that now, more than ever before, we are being issued with a warning that we can no longer ignore; a reminder to stop taking all of this for granted and of the paradoxical nature of humankind, comparatively insignificant amongst life on earth and yet with phenomenal destructive power. Pope Francis in his Encyclical *Laudato si'* (2015) lays out the Christian basis for a duty of care for our common home, warning of 'extreme weather events' to come; the past year has demonstrated this with particular clarity as storm after storm rips through the countryside on every continent and temperatures swing at what can only be considered an alarming rate. Rejecting the need to protect and preserve the environment seems to me like rejecting again the Garden of Eden; once lost, it can only be remembered with nostalgia and longing.

Yet despite the efforts of the Pope five years ago, the question of whether it is possible to be both religious and an environmentalist is still repeated, as if an answer other than, 'OF COURSE! WHY ON EARTH NOT?' is, if not necessarily expected, at least something that might not be altogether surprising. Well, I think the question itself is astonishing, and I can hardly believe that religious communities of the West show very little interest in actively dispelling this myth. Even

Catholic churches in this country are not particularly bothered with embracing the cause and using their unique platform to educate what are often very large congregations. Instead, we pray for victims of freak weather conditions without seeming to notice that, as the old saying goes, prevention is better than cure, and in this case quite a lot can actually be done to preserve the futures of millions of vulnerable, and usually socioeconomically disadvantaged peoples. For example, the super typhoon Haiyan which hit the Philippines in 2013 killed at least 6300 people; the negative effects on the poor as the climate becomes increasingly unstable will only increase.

For someone of an older generation, this five-year period may seem too short to expect anything to have changed anyway, but I think that for someone of my generation, five years is a long time, with much potential for positive changes to be realised. Looking at such a time period as a recent graduate, my life so far has been divided into even smaller educational blocks, each seeing huge changes in maturity and intellectual development, particularly over the last four years of Uni. I have changed so much over those years and so much has been done, that the idea of five years of apparent inaction is a problem, and I don't necessarily think this is just the result of youthful naivety. Perhaps this appreciation of time is something that young people can offer to the discussion, averting the temporal complacency of the old.

A bit about me

I grew up in a beautiful valley in Gloucestershire, surrounded by nature. Throughout my childhood I spent hours outdoors, walking in the fields, swimming in the sea and rivers. We visited West Wales at least once a year for as long as I can remember, and there are pictures of me dipping my wriggling baby toes into the sea from my mother's arms. There is something about the coast in that area which has a sort of spiritual power.

Perhaps it is the liminality of it, the point between solid land and the wild, restless waves, where you can lie on your stomach in the tough, slippery, almost buoyant grass and see nothing before and below you except the water, hearing its gurgling murmurs or raging crash. That feeling of security and exhilaration is hard to match. I am not alone in feeling the power of this landscape; the antiquarian Sir Richard Colt Hoare wrote in 1793 'No place could ever be more suited to retirement, contemplation or Druidical mysteries, surrounded by inaccessible rock and open to a wide expanse of ocean.'[1] Prehistoric settlements are visible in the circular foundations of stony huts and a Neolithic burial chamber is visible where the earth meets the sky, a clear focal point for approaching visitors. The attraction of the place continued into the Christian era, with chapels and churches clinging to the coastline beside holy wells and the ruins of places associated with saints. In the twelfth century it was declared that two pilgrimages here were the equivalent of one to Rome. In addition, the whole area is studded with saints' names, St John's Point, St Bride's Bay, St Justinian's, St Non's Well, St George's Channel. My immersion in this world has certainly influenced my understanding of Christianity, through this almost idealised Celtic version. I believe that the strong sense of the wild godliness of nature within me is inspired by this vision of the aliveness of the landscape as God created it.

The monastery where we occasionally attended Mass was set on the green slopes of a similar valley. You would often see deer and foxes through the morning mist and hear birds singing their hearts out in the sun. Thus, from my earliest childhood, the idea of separating God from creation and nature was pretty much unthinkable. 'The Holy Spirit is the air we breathe.' These beautiful words heard in a sermon from Glenstal Abbey, Co. Limerick, Republic of Ireland, capture something of what this connection means to me, of the aliveness of God and the flowing life force that sustains us at the very centre of our being, through our breath. I like to think of this when out walking, imagining this aspect of God flowing through me with every lungful, so much cleaner in the English countryside than in so many parts of the world. It concerns and terrifies me that, as a society, we are moving away from knowing what it is to breathe fresh air, or to see the multitude of stars stretched across the night sky, as we fill our world with pollution of every kind. But what surprises me the most is that not all Christians in the West seem to realise that concern for the environment is more than some trendy way to gain applause with the most superficial of actions. If we believe that God created the world and is in every atom that constitutes it, this concern is a fundamental obligation to the creation and life given to us by God. At least for me, some of the times I have felt closest to God have been when alone with my thoughts on a cliff, or wild swimming, or listening to the music of the birds on a hilltop. God, for me, whether in the raging autumn storm or the stillness of a spring evening, is a sensory experience.

Perception of Christianity and environmentalism

Yet, surprisingly to me, this failure of Christianity has been the case throughout history. Indeed, it has been blamed for the current worldwide attitude of complacency to the environment, citing a passage in the book of Genesis which seems to justify human exploitation of the natural world; 'And God said, Let us make man in our image, after our likeness: and let them have dominion over the fish of the sea, and over the fowl of the air and over the cattle and over all the earth and over every creeping thing that creepeth upon the earth' (Genesis 1.26). If one takes into consideration the persecution by the earliest Christians of the native religions of Britain and Europe, revolving around worship of the land, it seems a plausible claim that the Christian church in the West has been designed from the beginning to assert itself over nature. It is these sorts of ideas that allow the question of whether you can be both Christian and an environmentalist to circulate still. In a recent instalment of the 'Christian Comment' in my local newspaper the Methodist minister admitted the need for the church as a whole to review how teachings on the environment are interpreted, suggesting it should be seen as an integral part of our life, analogous to the doctrine of the Trinity, to shift from a perception of humanity as superior, to seeing ourselves as an equal part of the whole eco-system. It is time for us to rethink what was meant in that word 'dominion'.

How is it, I asked myself, that this single interpretation of a short passage in the Bible can be used to associate Christians with culpability for the current state of the environment? It may feel unfair, but it is not actually possible to deny that this is how some Christians do interpret those words. You only have to look at the street preachers in many cities, who expose Christianity to the ridicule of every well-educated person who hears them as they deny evolution, or to the climate change denying Christians of Trump's America, to see that people do actively take a narrowly 'human dominance' approach. This is certainly contrary to the writings of early Christian theologians such as Aquinas, who frequently emphasised the inseparability of God and all living creations: 'Since God is very being by His own essence... as long as a thing has being, God must be present... But being is innermost in each thing... Hence it must be that God is in all things, and innermostly' (*Summa Theologica*

I, Question 8, Article 1). Perhaps this connection has been lost amid the advances of the Industrial Revolution and the urbanisation that resulted, leading to a larger portion of the population living without contact with nature, in a world where insects and mud are avoided with screams. I can see how with a literalist reading, the creation story could be interpreted as explicitly authorising complete exploitation of the natural environment for the good, or apparent good at least, of humans, but why is that still going unchallenged by church leaders?

It may be true, then, that Christianity has, at least through passivity, played a role in how the environment is now treated, and as such the Church does need to take a stronger stance on the issue. It is not productive or fair, however, to hold a religion entirely to blame for the admittedly appalling ignorance that current world leaders seem determined to demonstrate, in complete opposition to the arguments of scientists. It is tempting to create a scapegoat when upset and angry, yet if real change is to take place it must be through uniting all the various groups, in humility over the failings of the past, that share in the joy and beauty of the world, who rely on nature for their existence, rather than seeking to alienate any individual one. It seems to me that if anyone truly desires change for the better, it is essential that we unite, as Christians, scientists and politicians, behind our common cause and leave the past behind us. I believe the motivations that ensure the climate crisis remains a topic largely avoided on the political soap box and in the religious pulpit transcend the bounds of any religious creed, reflecting instead the strong human desire to hide from anything quite this scary. What we need to do now is wholeheartedly to face this terrifying reality.

Cause for hope

What I think is clear, and actually very exciting, is that there is a huge scope for Christian churches to influence the attitude of a large body of the population. The church has a unique platform for advancing social reform, and it could be using it to address the issues that politicians shy away from. It seems to me that in order to have any credibility in the modern world, and in order to restore its esteem and attract a new generation, it had better start doing so soon. Moreover, I think the church might well claim that it holds a responsibility to actively educate people in what is right and this, as in any area of attainment to excellence, must involve using the best evidence available. Despite this, I rarely see any preacher being really courageous and pushing the limits of a congregation. Rather, the same old sermons are recycled, preaching to the converted and pandering to their arrogances. As it stands, I think that amongst my peers it is largely Christianity's hypocrisy when it comes to morality that makes them question why they should take it seriously since they can abide by a moral code of their own with less contradictory results.

I have not quite given up hope yet, however, as there are a few encouraging instances of church leaders putting in some effort. Pope Francis demonstrates his willingness to embrace science in the opening remarks of the *Laudato si'* where he grounds his comments on the 'best scientific knowledge available' to us. The fact that for many commentators this is worth mentioning indicates that this has not always been the case, but it is a relief to see the pontiff willing to change what has gone before.

Although unrelated to the environment, I recently saw an example of exactly how the church can use its unique platform for political ends, with the real power to alter people's mindsets. I usually find readings about compassion and loving one's neighbour somewhat frustrating, because, in my experience, preachers repeatedly refuse to say more than some sloppy, un-concrete babble about 'love', whilst being too afraid to offend anyone with strong guidance about what exactly it means to love in a real, aggressive, powerful way. Yet on this occasion, in the context of such readings, I witnessed the very real courage required to venture outside of the remit of a Christian priest's literal and narrow-minded reading, and to make a political statement. The political issue was the then current news item concerning the Islamic State bride Shamima Begum and her right, or otherwise, to British citizenship. According to an opinion poll, 78% of Brits support her citizenship being revoked. The priest argued against this, saying that we have a responsibility to such people and to deny them achieves nothing. It must have taken some courage, and he risked alienating a sizeable portion of the community. Yet despite this, he chose to use his position in the pulpit to argue for something he believed to be right. Who can know how many minds he changed, but at least he had the courage to try. Putting this active Christianity into practice is the kind of action which merits the respect of those who would otherwise be sceptical. It is statements such as those of the Pope and this parish priest that encourage the respect of the non-religious community and foster my hope. What we need now is for a strong centralised stance of the Churches in this country, to lobby government and educate congregations.

In many ways it seems to me that the frequent refusal of the church to take a strong position in social matters such as this is part of what alienates many of my friends from Christianity. And this ethical timidity stems in significant part, I think, from the Church's intractable theological conservatism – a conservatism which is difficult to stomach for those who have developed a much more liberal moral outlook. Social justice has no hope without political support; therefore, churches must speak out on politics. Wasn't Jesus political? He would not otherwise have been crucified. The church cannot expect to be taken seriously unless it takes on such great moral issues as climate change.

In the period 2016–2020, British politics has been completely wrapped up in the business of Brexit, which has, as it were, drowned out the voices of groups such as Extinction Rebellion and the inspiring teenage Swede Greta Thunberg. It is a fact that we are currently facing a climate crisis, yet I do not recall this featuring more than once or twice in church, in the prayers or sermon. Is the church so very introspective that it cannot see that the human disasters faced as the result of natural ones are not coincidental or random? How, if the church cares for humans, does it not see that it has to promote care for the environment as well? It is all very well to argue that humankind was given dominion over all the creatures of the earth, but this won't be such a laugh when we have destroyed the earth itself. For me, one of the most distressing aspects of the church's apparent apathy about this is that, on the whole, when you do hear about a church group with environmental concerns at its heart, it rarely includes the senior, older members of the community; it is the young who are concerned for their futures. Once again, this is not confined to church leaders but is generally the case for the older generations against whom it can seem like a constant battle to demand attention.

Preparing for this essay, I discovered that the Church of England appoints a bishop in the House of Lords as an ambassador for the environment. Who knew? I do not claim to be an expert, but I certainly did not. What has that bishop been doing in his role? The holder of that portfolio changes from time to time and therefore the responsibility is shared. To be fair to him, even committed environmental activists agree that the current situation stems from 30 years of failed campaigning by their own members, but these are mostly people with no political leverage beyond their right to vote and to protest, which surely does not apply to a Bishop in the House of Lords. Digging around on the internet, one can find various articles he has written on the subject, but nothing in national newspapers, no change to laws, or any meaningful difference. The General Synod has debated the issue of the environment without there being any indication of radical change.

Perhaps it is unfair to expect visible alterations. After all, what can a church really do beyond changing to a green energy supplier and recycling their service sheets? I'm afraid these cursory measures are simply not enough, and the solution, it seems to me, comes down to the unique opportunity churches have to create a community united by a shared passion and belief, to use words to join people together, to create a community with the power to act, to pressurise governments not just in the UK but around the world. As Ridley says in E.M. Forster's *Maurice*, 'Words *are* deeds'. I believe it comes down to church leaders being able to mobilise this energy, raise awareness and guide the community to where efforts should be focussed. What could be more powerful than the entire religious community uniting to demand greater respect for the world? And what better way for the church to regain some credibility in relation to social justice than by addressing this matter, which should be at the forefront of our collective consciousness? It would be the evidence I need that churches are more than exclusive clubs and that they can actually mobilise to promote matters of huge human significance.

It comes down to convincing action guided by words of wisdom.

If the Christian church is still interested in evangelism, it is time for a change in its strategy – away from the old tale of 'come to us and be saved' to a practical agenda of living by Jesus' ethical insights. Salvation is no longer the most compelling argument for Christianity and I think this explains much of the reason behind the general shift away from religion in First World countries, stemming from the increased feeling of security and safety which replaces a need for a religion offering those things. The Church must move away from using fear, almost as a bribe, to lure people in. It needs to prove that religion is not just about a Sunday obligation to attend church and feel self-righteously better about ourselves. Instead, it has to offer rigorous engagement with issues of human rights and social justice in the context of the beautiful music, ancient Mass settings and of course the biblical teaching to love and respect others. Part of this is to identify what we want the world to be and to do what we can to make it an achievable reality. I think it is through the evidence of such actions that people may be convinced Christianity has the power to lead to good and might therefore be worth exploring.

The advantages of this would go multiple ways; apart from it being in the interests of the church, and how it is perceived, to take a strong position on a subject such as environmentalism, the environmental movement could be massively aided by the wholehearted involvement of religious groups. Unlike individual governments, the pervasion of the five major religions of the world could facilitate the spread of environmental interest and awareness across political borders. Even should it only be the Christian church, this movement would be phenomenal and potentially of enormous significance. The time has passed in which it might have been acceptable to pass climate change off as not relevant to a religious context, and heads must be removed from the sand. What we need to do is have the courage to really look this issue in the face and start thinking in the long term. Each of us is responsible for the outcome of this momentous battle and it is time that religious leaders began living up to, and taking seriously, the positions of trust and enormous influence they occupy.

In the context of considering the no-religion identity of my generation, my conclusion is that we find religion, and the Church in particular, has its priorities wrong, and indeed is struggling to identify what they are in the first place. My concern has been specifically about its feeble response to the most challenging moral problem of our age, our abuse of the environment, but *a fortiori*, I think my contemporaries find themselves disillusioned by the Church's perceived attitude to a raft of social issues: enjoying yourself, politics, sexual ethics, intellectual rigour to name but a few. In short; being out of touch and, crucially, too afraid to engage energetically to address any of them.

Notes

1   *The journeys of Sir Richard Colt Hoare through Wales and England, 1793–1810* by Sir Richard Colt Hoare; published by A. Sutton (Gloucester) in 1983 edited by M.W. Thompson, p. 48.

Does Religion Still Have a Future?

By Brian Mountford

Considering how to frame this last chapter, I decided it needs to be less of a summing up and more a question of where we go from here. But first, one might look at the flip side of one of the implicit premises of several of the chapters. I speak for myself and not for the other contributors when I say I have assumed that the figure of 70% of the 18–24s having no religion is a worrying statistic rather than a neutral one, no doubt because I have been a Christian priest for most of my life. It might also appear that I am trying to rescue religion at all costs with arguments that religion is always there under the surface. If I flip that on its head, no-religion becomes an indication of a changed and enlightened attitude towards religion, which is now a minority interest. Attitudes to religion have changed radically in the West. Christianity has been inextricably embedded in Western politics, morality, land ownership, education, hospitals, literature, art and music for centuries. Its privilege has been slowly diminishing, arguably, since the Enlightenment, but during the past thirty or forty years that unravelling has accelerated exponentially. In a secular, multicultural society this should be regarded as liberating because the freedom of belief is paramount and in an inclusive society it is important to be as non-discriminatory towards religion as it is towards race, gender, culture, or sexual orientation. The result is that there is a strong case for speaking of a 'post-Christian' society in the secular West.

In my introductory chapter I made much of the idea that no-religion is connected primarily with the widespread ignorance of religious belief and practice in present day Western Society leading to a kind of inevitable indifference. While that assessment seems true of popular culture, I think it is inaccurate with regard to learning and scholarship, in which a significant proportion of the population is, or has been, engaged at one level or another. It might be the case that most contemporary undergraduates studying Reformation history have never been to a Mass, or, studying English literature, are unfamiliar with the biblical stories, but they do not claim to be ideologically against learning about religion. They look at it objectively as a cultural phenomenon, without necessarily thinking its claims demand a response from them: the Bible, the Christian creeds, and what historically people have thought and believed about them are in many contexts fascinating and on a par with other ancient texts, philosophies, and practices.

Unsurprisingly things are not black and white even on the flip side. It is no accident that many people speak of being 'spiritual but *not religious*', although I haven't established whether many young people use that phrase. I have italicised *not religious* because that suggests it is religion that is unpalatable, not contemplating a spiritual dimension. And *spiritual* has very wide terms of reference. What is meant, I think, is such people are occasionally surprised by a need to find ways of looking at the world which transcend the values of a consumerist, trivialising culture. They have an interest in what the theologian Paul Tillich called 'ultimate questions': Who am I? What's life about? Is there a Big Truth? It is easy to confuse antipathy towards religious institutions with indifference towards the spiritual. On the flip side of that, however, the theologian and psychotherapist Mark Vernon has suggested ours is a 'flat' society in which people are incapable of seeing through 'spiritual eyes' at all because they have neither the intuition nor the vocabulary. It is as if the unrelenting materialism that has driven an ever-increasing global population to pollute the seas, concrete over the fields, and allow free market economics to widen and widen the gap between rich and poor in a ruthlessly competitive and anxiety-inducing world of competition has deadened spiritual sensitivity. The spiritual dimension has faded because it no longer makes sense in a world community that is killing itself. This strikes me as an extreme view, but one to be taken into account.

I do not assume that readers are themselves religious, only that they find the phenomenon of religion worthy of picking up this book for.

So where do we go from here? What is the future of religion?

However analytical you are, foretelling the future is an uncertain science. The late Dick Chorley, Professor of geography at Sidney Sussex College, Cambridge, was an expert on weather before satellite technology had become as sophisticated as it is today and when we used to ask him how it would turn out tomorrow, he'd reply with a wry grin that most probably it would be the same as today. Statistics bore him out.

1. Take a global rather than northern hemisphere view.

When it comes to the prospects for religion, one might reasonably expect the future to bring more of the same: the slow decline of Christianity in the West, with occasional trend-bucking exceptions in cathedrals and conservative evangelical communities, and pockets of vibrant Islam and Hinduism within the ethnic communities of certain major towns and cities. At the same time, worldwide, Islam is growing fast and is expected to reach numerically the same size as Christianity (30%) by 2050. One can expect the expansion of Christianity in African and Chinese churches, not least as a factor of their population growth. And when it comes to more-of-the-same, it is hard to see religious fundamentalism compromising with western liberal values, particularly when it underpins a conservative political state like Saudi Arabia, Iran, or the 'Bible Belt' in the United States of America.

2. Did COVID-19 reveal anything about the future for religion?

Since self-giving and compassion are at the core of most theologies, I have always expected religion to respond well to a crisis. In extreme situations, people often turn to religion for stability, in search of values that transcend the miseries and challenges of a crisis. After 9/11 churches filled up for *ad hoc* acts of prayer, reflection and expressions of deeply concerned fellow-feeling. This sacred space the churches offered was an existing resource and a natural place in which to ritualise feelings of vulnerability, compassion and moral outrage.

When the COVID-19 virus struck, church communities rallied round to shop for older people and got on the telephone to give support and encouragement especially to those on their own. But during lockdown, because of social distancing rules, sacred space was denied and worship went online. Suddenly religion lost one of its greatest assets – the stage on which instinctual religious response can be enacted in the way it was after 9/11 or is at Christmas time in carol services. These are moments when religious doctrine is secondary to religious ritual, when the raw religious response of crying out for mercy and help can turn into hope.

So, the closure of churches during the COVID-19 pandemic exposed a weakness that religion cannot survive without people meeting for company, worship and ritual. Some of that dynamic was transferred online, via *Zoom*, but it wasn't the same. Although pre-recorded services and podcasts attracted far more hits than the numbers who would normally attend worship. It was easy to skip the bits you found boring or didn't like, you could watch it when you wanted, didn't have to pay for parking, and didn't have to put money in the collection.

Many commentators have suggested that the shock of COVID-19 and the way it has forced us to give up many things we take for granted, forcing us to live more simply, will have a long-lasting effect. When it is all over there will be a 'new normal', a kinder, less greedy, more altruistic approach to life. I hope this might be the case and I can see possible parallels between post COVID-19 and the post Second World War period when people who had suffered deprivations during that time were content just to be at peace, send their children to school, and put a meal on the table.

Judging from breaches of COVID-19 discipline, however, with people gathering for parties and breaking self-isolation rules, it looks like the selfish gene is likely to prevail. But there's no doubt that testing experiences do encourage people to take moral stock. That's why fasting, the hair shirt, pilgrimage, and sacrificial giving of time and money to others in need plays such an important part in spiritual life.

3. Science and the Academy will make further discoveries which challenge traditional doctrine.

There's nothing new in that. Religion has faced plenty of paradigm shifting challenges before: Galileo, Newton, Darwin, Freud, Textual Criticism (of 'sacred' texts), the sexual revolution. In a sense what is there that scientific or philosophical step changes can do to religion that they haven't done already? The genie is out of the bottle. And this creates a dilemma for organised religion: to face the fact or pretend it never happened.

For the Christian religion with its back to the wall of tradition, facing the secularism of the West, there's a deep-seated reluctance to engage with prevailing intellectual or ethical trends for fear that its theological foundations will be shaken. Much safer to be proudly counter-cultural and justify your position on the grounds that moral and intellectual trends are here today and gone tomorrow, whereas ancient teachings, embedded in divine texts, transcend time. The trouble is, anyone who takes the trouble to read about the history of the Bible will realise the whole system of Christian doctrine is a human construct with a history as much influenced by politics as spiritual insight, and that the Bible by no means always supports orthodox doctrine. In his award-winning book, *A History of the Bible*, John Barton shows there is little backing in the New Testament for the central Christian doctrine of the Holy Trinity, which claims that Father, Son and Holy Spirit are co-equal parts of the Godhead. This has been known to biblical scholars for two hundred years yet remains unfamiliar to most Christians. And so, the Christian response to modernity is strained; there's a dissonance between the world of religious belief and the world of modern knowledge, which clergy and religious leaders find difficult to solve and to come to terms with. Consequently, in the popular view, all Christianity is assumed to be a literalist version of itself: science seems to oppose it, it seems ethically out-of-date, and, in the word of one of its greatest critics, delusional.

Saying that, I am aware that I do an injustice to a large number of thinking Christians, including congregations that I have ministered to, who recognise, for example, that science and religion are compatible because they both search for truth and understanding of the universe, and I think the (sometimes unintentional) anti-intellectualism on the part of the Church leadership simply acknowledges that the main challenge to religions *is* intellectual. But when it comes to the crunch, the Church is inclined to hide its head under the duvet. It hates listening to criticism, blithely assumes it possesses the truth, is scared the bottom might fall out of its ark, and, because the clergy are psychologically (and professionally, in the sense that promotion depends on it) in bondage to orthodoxy, they are frightened to let doctrine be in dialogue with twenty-first-century thinking. Do they also think their congregations will be bored by the engagement and find it too dry? But people (and especially young people) want to be allowed to think for themselves and rather than taking pride in being counter-cultural, religion needs to be more enculturated, engaged with things as they are rather than with things as they were.

Which is not to say religion needs to compromise with secular society, or be reductionist, or not to test contemporary secular assumptions. Religions need to have a robust and open debate with society, being willing to give and take in the cut and thrust of discussion, recognising that it certainly doesn't possess the whole truth. You might object that 'society' just isn't interested, but my experience is different, and I find a widespread fascination with the philosophy of religion and meaning-of-life questions.

4. Will the future of religion be Multifaith?

During the past forty years the expansion of international governance, global stock markets, and the mass culture created by information technology, together with cheap and easy means of movement of people around the cities of the world, has led to cultural traditions that were once localised and national being intermingled. This has included changing attitudes to religion. Whereas Christianity was once the hallmark of Britain and its Empire, now varieties of different religions are seen at firsthand as part of everyday life. Muslim men returning from Friday worship wearing a white kaftan and kufi hat is a common sight in many British cities; the festivals of Hanukkah, Eid, Diwali, and Christmas (for example) are recognised and given equal standing. Local Councils of Religion have grown up to show that people of different religions can work together in harmony and to demonstrate that acts of extreme political religious fundamentalism are the exception rather than the rule for religions which have at their heart peace and love of neighbour.

This has led to a notion of inclusive religion under the banner of 'Multifaith', in which equal opportunity, non-discrimination, and mutuality of faiths is key. The idea appeals to secularists and humanists because they see that by not privileging any one religious tradition, they are marginalising all religions while seeming to be scrupulously objective and socially on message.

When the students of St Hilda's College, Oxford, were asked to choose between a Christian chapel or a multifaith space, the majority opted for multifaith space because it seemed fair.

But there's a weakness in the argument. Multifaith is really a sociopolitical idea about religious toleration, freedom of speech, and freedom to worship, not an idea motivated from within religions themselves. Religions are not intrinsically inclined to be multifaith: they want to hold tight to their culture and beliefs and celebrate them, not to water them down into some sort of thin syncretic soup. Giles Fraser has written on the British news website *Unherd* that 'religion has never been tempted by anything approaching Esperanto because the generalised form of religion evacuates it of any meaning. In all serious religious traditions, the universal is rooted within the specific. Yes, there are still those who think the multi faith space is all about wanting the world to sing in perfect harmony, all religions together, brother and sisters in arms.'

So, while I am glad when different religions and cultures work together for the common good, I do not see multifaith as being particularly significant for the future of religion itself. Any such life-giving heartbeat must be in something more ancient and subtle. What is it?

5. Do we still need religion?

It depends how you define it, what you think religion is. In my opening essay I used two standard definitions: the OED's 'belief in and worship of a superhuman controlling power, especially a personal God or gods', and Émile Durkheim's 'a unified system of beliefs and practices relative to sacred things'. Now I want briefly to explore a broader view which sees religion in terms of

a) understanding the self,

b) prioritising ethical values, especially how we relate to one another personally, nationally, and globally, and

c) a sense of the sacred deriving from the idea that values are more than our invention.

This view of religion draws on part of John Hunt's book *Bringing God up to Date* (JHP, 2021). He suggests that humans began to think and act religiously as they became self-aware and faced the dilemmas self-awareness created – an insight captured in the Genesis creation story, as well as in the foundational stories of some other religions. In the Garden of Eden, Adam and Eve are at one with nature seeing life as 'it', but as soon as 'me' comes into the equation things begin to go wrong: they enjoy the fruits of self-awareness – sex, love, and relationship – but also have to face separation and death and the fact that the self in the long run is self-destructive. Religions grew to help us see the *other*, to connect, and recognise a larger truth. Religion helps us to control the appetites of self and encourages service to the common good. It's a view also propounded by the classical Athenian philosophers Socrates, Plato, and Aristotle with their ideas of happiness being based on living a good life, i.e., a moral life. Socrates said that an unexamined life is not worth living; Plato, that the virtuous man is the happy man; and, taking up the Platonic theme, Aristotle argued that happiness and virtue go hand in hand and are related to a person's ability to fulfil their potential.

John Hunt says a well-grounded religion creates structures that control the appetites of the self, provides a vision of a good life, and a moral code to frame it – a 'means of transcending our biology'. It does this by providing the framework for relating to each other through rituals and with stories which act as touchstones for this moral and spiritual journey. If we didn't have religion, we would need something close to it. 'And in the hole left in the twentieth century by the ebbing belief in God, we have tried a number of different ideas, organising ourselves around race (fascism), country (nationalism), production (communism), consumption (capitalism) – ideas that don't seem to have worked.' And the reason they have not worked is probably because they are based on *us* rather than on the *other*.

The *other* is a word that can stand not only for all those persons who are not *me*, but also for something absolute and universal – the Sacred. A prime example is the intuitive sense that values must be more than our invention. In other words, ethics is not merely culturally relative, but relies on absolute moral imperatives, which might be specific, such as torture is universally wrong, or more generalised, like Plato's sovereignty of Good, or Jesus' sovereignty of love. Religion, or our sense of the *sacred*, nurtured through awe and wonder, has evolved in the human psyche over tens of thousands of years to the point where it is hardwired into the human brain. 'We have a hunger for the meaning we describe in religion,' says Hunt, 'for the stories that bind us together, that tell us where we came from and where we're going, that explain how we should relate to each other and the world around us, like we have a hunger for food and relationship.'

Conclusion

I recognise that the values of self-giving, seeing the other, and reaching for absolute value in a precarious existence on an endangered planet, admired here by Hunt, are reached just as easily by people who profess no religious interest or affiliation, but the argument here is that such interests are intrinsically religious whether their proponent thinks so or not. Hunt says at one point that religion is primary. 'So much so that many deeply religious cultures don't even have a word for it.' I think this is what is meant by those who describe themselves as spiritual but not religious and all those who say they don't believe in God, but miss him, or describe themselves as devoutly sceptical.

It seems to me that the essays in this book, while not setting out to define what religion is or to defend the so called 'no-religion' of their age group, throw considerable light on the claim made in this final section that religious questioning and contemplation of values is hardwired into the human psyche and won't go away. So, religion won't disappear any time soon, even if church attendance continues to decline or the wearing of traditional religious dress becomes less common, or states forbid religious observance. Worldwide, religion remains massively influential. That very fact highlights that there is 'good' and 'bad' religion. Religion which seeks to promote love, the common good, and understanding of the ultimate meaning of life; religion enforcing political power through corruption and violence; religion presenting its spirituality openly and critically; religion trying to brainwash its followers with fundamentalist hogwash; religion promoting justice; religion oppressing women or persecuting homosexuals. So often religions find it difficult to honour the beliefs and teachings they promote and that is a turn-off, not only to the young.

CHRISTIAN ALTERNATIVE
BOOKS

THE NEW OPEN SPACES

Throughout the two thousand years of Christian tradition there
have been, and still are, groups and individuals that exist in
the margins and upon the edge of faith. But in Christianity's
contrapuntal history it has often been these outcasts and
pioneers that have forged contemporary orthodoxy out
of former radicalism as belief evolves to engage with and
encompass the ever-changing social and scientific realities. Real
faith lies not in the comfortable certainties of the Orthodox,
but somewhere in a half-glimpsed hinterland on the dirt track
to Emmaus, where the Death of God meets the Resurrection,
where the supernatural Christ meets the historical Jesus,
and where the revolution liberates both the oppressed and
the oppressors.

Welcome to Christian Alternative... a space at the edge where
the light shines through.
If you have enjoyed this book, why not tell other readers by
posting a review on your preferred book site.
Recent bestsellers from Christian Alternative are:

Bread Not Stones
The Autobiography of An Eventful Life
Una Kroll
The spiritual autobiography of a truly remarkable woman
and a history of the struggle for ordination in the Church of
England.
Paperback: 978-1-78279-804-0 ebook: 978-1-78279-805-7

The Quaker Way
A Rediscovery
Rex Ambler
Although fairly well known, Quakerism is not well understood.
The purpose of this book is to explain how Quakerism works as
a spiritual practice.
Paperback: 978-1-78099-657-8 ebook: 978-1-78099-658-5

Blue Sky God
The Evolution of Science and Christianity
Don MacGregor
Quantum consciousness, morphic fields and blue-sky
thinking about God and Jesus the Christ.
Paperback: 978-1-84694-937-1 ebook: 978-1-84694-938-8

Celtic Wheel of the Year
Tess Ward
An original and inspiring selection of prayers combining
Christian and Celtic Pagan traditions, and interweaving their
calendars into a single pattern of prayer for every morning
and night of the year.
Paperback: 978-1-90504-795-6

Christian Atheist

Belonging without Believing

Brian Mountford

Christian Atheists don't believe in God but miss him: especially the transcendent beauty of his music, language, ethics, and community.

Paperback: 978-1-84694-439-0 ebook: 978-1-84694-929-6

Compassion Or Apocalypse?

A Comprehensible Guide to the Thought of René Girard

James Warren

How René Girard changes the way we think about God and the Bible, and its relevance for our apocalypse-threatened world.

Paperback: 978-1-78279-073-0 ebook: 978-1-78279-072-3

Diary Of A Gay Priest

The Tightrope Walker

Rev. Dr. Malcolm Johnson

Full of anecdotes and amusing stories, but the Church is still a dangerous place for a gay priest.

Paperback: 978-1-78279-002-0 ebook: 978-1-78099-999-9

Do You Need God?

Exploring Different Paths to Spirituality Even For Atheists

Rory J.Q. Barnes

An unbiased guide to the building blocks of spiritual belief.

Paperback: 978-1-78279-380-9 ebook: 978-1-78279-379-3

Readers of ebooks can buy or view any of these bestsellers by clicking on the live link in the title. Most titles are published in paperback and as an ebook. Paperbacks are available in traditional bookshops. Both print and ebook formats are available online.

Find more titles and sign up to our readers' newsletter at http://www.johnhuntpublishing.com/christianity
Follow us on Facebook at
https://www.facebook.com/ChristianAlternative